Every Man a Brother

EVERY MAN A BROTHER

BY WILLIAM F. DRUMMOND

With a foreword by John F. Cronin

CORPUS BOOKS
Washington—Cleveland

Corpus Instrumentorum, Inc.
1330 Massachusetts Ave., N.W.
Washington, D.C. 20005

First Printing 1968

Library of Congress Catalog Card Number: 68–10449

PRINTED IN THE UNITED STATES OF AMERICA

FOREWORD

One of the very important legacies of Vatican Council II is the new sophistication acquired by many theologians and moralists. Not too long ago most Catholic scholars considered major Roman documents, such as encyclicals and solemn addresses, as being almost divinely inspired. Comment and criticism uniformly consisted, with few exceptions, of a careful spelling out of the precise meaning of the Pontiff's words, with little attention to the underlying historical and doctrinal background.

By contrast, most writers today realize that papal utterances are generally only the final stage in a process of doctrinal development and refinement. A critical element in this process is the study of problems by scholars throughout the world, as they seek a consensus consonant with divine revelation, natural law, and the traditions of the Church.

Father Drummond's book is such a study. He examines

critically, in the light of natural law, the major social encyclicals, addresses, and writings of the modern era. Where pertinent, he brings in the conclusions of Vatican Council II. The result is a well-rounded and balanced analysis of the major topics under consideration.

These topics should interest serious students of social problems. The author commences his study with a careful analysis of the social encyclicals and natural law. This is followed by a treatment of the major institutions of society: property, social organizations, economic groups, the political state, and international bodies and programs. Under each heading there are abundant and relevant excerpts from the basic social writings of modern popes. The selections are well chosen and the commentary is judicious. The book concludes with an excellent reading list.

This carefully reasoned study is of obvious interest to Catholic students of social problems and to those whose concern is natural law. But this book could have an ecumenical impact as well. As Christians study together their origins and their divergences, there is real value in an explanation of how the Catholic Church's magisterium applies the doctrine of the natural law. Many Christians who are not in communion with Rome tend to an exclusively Scriptural basis for moral teaching. Father Drummond can help them to understand the Church's different perspective and the ways by which the social teaching of the Church is formed.

Those outside the Christian community can also find much that is of interest in these pages. It affords them a "behind-the-scenes" insight into an area of Catholic teaching which has won respect outside the Christian family.

Jewish thinkers share Catholic concern with the dignity of man as the basis of social ethic. So do many persons who have no formal religious beliefs. In a world that is increasingly open to dialogue, we have here material for valuable and interesting discussions.

JOHN F. CRONIN, S.S.
Department of Social Action
United States Catholic Conference

CONTENTS

9

Every Man a Brother

CHAPTER ONE

THE SOCIAL ENCYCLICALS AND NATURAL LAW

Pope John XXIII addressed the encyclical *Pacem in Terris* to "All Men of Good Will." In a sense this was a startling innovation; it was the first time that such a salutation had been used in the formal introduction of an encyclical. It was a gracious ecumenical gesture characteristic of Pope John, echoed by him in the opening message to Vatican Council II.[1] Yet it is a salutation that might well have been used in all the social encyclicals, for it would be a mistake to restrict the value of these documents to those who accept the authority of the Pope. Actually they provide a common platform for discussion among men of all faiths; the moral doctrine of the encyclicals pertaining to the socio-economic order is a natural moral law doctrine.

Obviously the sources of Catholic social doctrine are two: reason and revelation. Any reader of the social encyclicals must be struck by the constant association of these two, the law of the Gospel and the natural law, in all the principal arguments that are given. Further reflection leaves the impression that in fact it is principally through

an appeal to reason that the social encyclicals call for the
reformation of the social order, an impression confirmed
by the words of *Pacem in Terris:*

> The doctrinal principles outlined in this document derive
> from or are suggested by the requirements of human nature
> itself and are for the most part dictates of the natural law.
> They provide Catholics therefore with a vast field in which
> they can meet and come to an understanding both with
> Christians separated from this Apostolic See, and also with
> human beings who are not enlightened by faith in Jesus
> Christ, but who are endowed with the light of reason and
> with a natural and operative honesty. (No 157; encyclical
> hereafter identified as PT; see *Mater et Magistra*, no. 220,
> hereafter MM.)

And the reason for this insistence on natural law is
indicated in the first encyclical of Pius XII on the *Unity of
Human Society.* "Before all else," he writes, "it is certain that
the radical and ultimate cause of the evils we deplore in
modern society is the denial and rejection of a universal
norm of morality—we mean the disregard so common now-
adays and foregetfulness of the natural law itself, which
has its foundation in God, Almighty Creator and Father of
all, supreme and absolute law giver, all wise and just judge
of human actions" (*Summi Pontificatus* [SP], 28).

This emphasis on reason, nature, and the natural law
marks every argument of the encyclicals. The fundamental
truth on which the understanding of human life depends,
namely, that man is made for eternity, is not only a Christian dogma, but a truth, as Leo XIII points out in *Rerum
Novarum*, which we learned from nature itself as our teacher
(*Rerum Novarum*, 33; hereafter RN). The possession and use
of material goods on which the whole economic order hinges
is vindicated as a natural right by all the social encyclicals

and the arguments they adduce for it are all arguments of reason and the "most sacred law of Nature" (RN, 20; see *Quadragesimo Anno* [QA], 45; PT 21).

The double aspect of property, individual and social, stressed against the excesses of individualism, is derived from the fact that nature and God, as the author of nature, have ordained private ownership in order that through this institution material goods may come to the realization of their purpose which is the service of the entire human family. The principle of subsidiarity in social life, given as the antidote for both the anarchy of individualism and the absorption of totalitarianism, is proposed as a fixed and unshakable principle of social philosophy (QA, 79). Racial discrimination can in no way be justified since "all men are equal because of their natural dignity" (PT, 44). The unity of the international community is based on the fact that "its members are human beings all equal by virtue of their natural dignity" (PT, 132).

The Christian ideal proposed by the encyclicals, then, does not dispense with the requirements of the natural order. Rather, to quote Pius XII again, "the profession of Christian truth and fidelity to the fundamental tenets of the Catholic faith are indissolubly bound up with the sincere and constant assertion of human nature's most authentic and exalted values."[2]

Revelation tells us that salvation is attained through union by grace with Christ; the union of all with Christ in the Kingdom of the Father. But while that kingdom will be perfectly realized only in eternity, it is built on this earth through human activities sanctified in Christ. All that is human, without losing its human character, becomes through grace the means of salvation. The Christian order is, in the words of the same pontiff, the order in which grace and nature converge. The divine law that governs man includes both what is directly and positively revealed by God to man and what man indirectly knows through the reasonable examination of the exigencies of his own nature. The natural law and the positive divine law are both emanations of the one eternal law of God. There is no contradiction between them, nor does one cancel out the other.

Thus our supernatural vocation in Christ is the framework within which we are to realize to the full the potentialities of our nature. The supernatural destiny of man assumes the whole order of nature; it does not destroy it. It is true that grace does not evolve from nature; but grace and nature do have an existential relationship. Grace, Pope Pius XII tells us,[3] is a new element inserted in the order of creation and of nature to perfect it and surpass it, giving supernatural aid for its better understanding and supernatural strength for its observance.

In the moral life of man, therefore, there are certain duties which man can know only through revelation: such are the obligations of faith, of membership in the Church, of the reception of the sacraments as means of grace. There are certain truths, too, affecting man's moral life, the knowledge of which depends on revelation: for instance, the necessity of the aid of supernatural grace for any meritorious act and the necessity of grace even for the constant fulfillment of the natural law itself.

There are other and more numerous duties, however, which reason itself can discover. Among these are men's duties in the economic, social, and political orders. Revelation gives no new system of economic or political life. Grace is necessary that man's activities in these fields be super-naturalized, but grace does not change the substance of those activities. Rather it supposes their natural goodness. The conformity of such activity with the demands of reason—with the natural law—is a condition of its elevation by grace.

In content, therefore, the moral demands of the socio-economic order of supernaturalized man are the demands of the natural law. The elevation of man gives a new finality to these demands: the realization of the Kingdom of Christ. It gives a new means to their fulfillment: the grace of Christ. And it gives a new motive for their observance: the charity of Christ. But in substance the rights and duties of man in the socio-economic order are derived from natural law, the outgrowth of the exigencies of his nature.

All these things are obvious to a careful reader of the social encyclicals. But it would appear from certain reactions to the publication of *Mater et Magistra* that a consequence of this natural law basis of Catholic social doctrine is not obvious. That consequence is the possibility, and the very necessity, of a development of that doctrine. It was the willingness of Pope John to accept the fact of the growing socialization of human life as "the fruit and expression of a natural tendency" and to propose guide lines for its development rather than reject it as a growth of socialism that caused certain ultra-conservatives to cry: "Mater, Si; Magistra, No."

This attitude derives from a misunderstanding of natural law. Natural law is not made up of formalistic prin-ciples devoid of content. Nor on the other hand is it a set of completely defined and codified rules which apply in the same way to every situation. It is rather a series of reason-

able precepts which are derived from a consideration of
the exigencies of human nature as that human nature
exists in concrete circumstances. Natural law doctrine,
correctly understood, is a balanced combination of essen-
tialism and existentialism which avoids the errors attendant
on the exaggeration of either.

Essentially considered, human nature is the same in
all men. Hence, certain universal principles of conduct can
be formulated which, in their abstract form, are immutable
and applicable to all men. The application of these principles is another matter. Applications are determined by
the concretely existing man. The universal principles will
find a different incidence and call for different specifications in different historical circumstances. Such specifications, as belonging to natural law, will still be generic
determinations, but they exhibit a developing content that
brings out new requirements of practical reason as they
meet the changing situation. Thus the source of natural
law is not merely the abstract nature of man but the concrete nature existing in a determined moment of history.

It is just such development that we find in the social
doctrine of the encyclicals *Rerum Novarum, Quadragesimo
Anno, Mater et Magistra,* and *Pacem in Terris.* The last two are
not a departure in teaching from their predecessors. There
is no sudden appearance here of what has been called
liberal catholicism. All four encyclicals treat of what is
known as the "social question": the question of the mutual
rights and duties of men in the socio-economic order; of
the right distribution of material goods; of the relationship between capital and labor, rich and poor, developed
and emerging nations.

Rerum Novarum and *Quadragesimo Anno* restrict themselves explicitly to this question in their opening paragraphs (RN, 3, 4; QA, 2). *Mater et Magistra*, after reviewing the teaching of these encyclicals, goes on to "exhort all . . . to draw from it inspiration and direction in the search for a solution of the social question adapted to our times" (QA, 50).

The central point of this "social question," Pius XII tells us (*Sertum Laetitiae*, 50), is that the goods of the earth created by God for all men should serve the use of all equitably, according to the principles of justice and charity. Here is the general principle of natural law that each of the encyclicals applies according to the needs of the time in which they were written.

At the time of *Rerum Novarum* the principal problem was the plight of the working man, the question of his fundamental rights as an individual that were denied to him under the harsh system of *laissez-faire*. The English title of the encyclical, "On the Condition of the Working Class," indicates its preoccupation with this phase of the social question.

To meet this particular problem *Rerum Novarum* stresses particularly four principles of social morality. The first of these is the right of private ownership. Against the extreme of socialism which would abolish it as the root of economic injustice, Leo XIII defended the natural right of ownership as the juridical foundaton of a just economic order. The inviolability of private property he calls the first and most fundamental principle for the alleviation of the condition of the masses.

Second, there is the right to a living wage. Against the complete freedom of contract held by the system of *laissez-faire*, Leo proclaimed the doctrine of the minimum just wage—the dictate of natural justice that wages must not be less than is sufficient to support a frugal and well-behaved working man.

Third, workers have the right to form labor unions. *Rerum Novarum* has well been called the magna carta of the labor movement in its defense of the natural right of working men to form associations within the state for their mutual aid and protection.

Fourth, the right of the state to intervene in the economic order must be admitted. Against the "hands off" policy of economic liberalism Leo XIII asserted the right and duty of the intervention of the state to protect the rights of the working man, to legislate with regard to conditions of work, hours of work, strikes, and so forth—an intervention limited by the requirements of the common good.

All these principles are reasserted and further developed by *Quadragesimo Anno, Mater et Magistra*, and *Pacem in Terris*. The problems which occasioned their assertion by *Rerum Novarum* did not end with the publication of that encyclical—they are still problems. But the years following *Rerum Novarum* saw changes in the socio-economic order that called for a further application of the natural law principles governing that order.

Quadragesimo Anno notes that *Rerum Novarum* had overthrown the principles of economic liberalism; that free competition on the *laissez-faire* model was dead, and that in its place we had the economic dictatorship of great corporations; that a new branch of jurisprudence—labor laws—had appeared to protect the rights of working men.

At the writing of *Quadragesimo Anno*, two things were threatening the correct solution of the social question: first, the growth of the power of the state: communism and fascism had made their appearance, and, in our own country, big government was emerging; and, second, class conflict between capital and labor which the encyclical calls "a grave evil of modern society."

The problem facing Pius XI forty years after *Rerum Novarum* was not the protection or assertion of the fundamental rights of the workers, but rather the reconstruction of the social order as a whole. Order and peaceful collaboration rather than conflict are necessary for the realization of social justice; and yet it must be an order which does not destroy the legitimate freedom of the members of society.

Against these dangers of the time—the extremes of the anarchy of class warfare and the regimentation of dictatorship—therefore, *Quadragesimo Anno* enunciated two further moral principles as the indispensable requisites of a properly structured social order: the concept of the organic structure of civil society, and the principle of subsidiarity.

According to the organic structure of society, civil society is made up of relatively autonomous lesser societies (organs, on the analogy of the human body), each of which contributes its function, the production of a certain good or service, for the common good of the whole. The various branches of economic life are just such organs—"orders" or vocational groups—with an inner principle of unity: the common good. Thus capital and labor are not opposed factions each struggling for the greatest share of the profits of enterprise; they are rather cooperating partners in the performance of a common function. Class warfare is incompatible with such a concept.

The principle of subsidiarity which Pius XI called a fixed and unshaken principle of social philosophy restricts the power of intervention of the state to necessary complementary activity.

Just as it is wrong to take from individuals what they can accomplish by their own initiative and industry to give to the community, so also it is an injustice and at the same time a grave evil and disturbance of right order to assign to a greater and higher association what lesser and subordinate organizations can do. For every social activity ought of its very nature to furnish help to the members of the social body, and never destroy and absorb them (QA, 79).

In 1961, at the time of the appearance of *Mater et Magistra*, the scene and consequent problems had again changed. This encyclical, more than any of the others, dwells on the tremendous changes that history has seen; changes which are enumerated in the fields of science and technology, and in the social and political fields, on national and international levels.

Because of these changes the scope of social justice must be enlarged; hence a new aspect is given to the fundamental social question. This new aspect finds expression in paragraph 122 of the encyclical:

the historical evolution of human affairs brings into ever greater relief the fact that the demands of justice and equity have a bearing not only on the relations between dependent working men and contractors or employers but also on the relation between different economic sectors, between areas economically more advanced and those that are underdeveloped within the same nation, and from a world point of view, on relations among countries at different stages of economic development.

The pressing problem now is not that of class warfare. It is interesting to see how the encyclical dismisses the Marxian myth of the necessity of class warfare by the simple appeal to the fact that class distinctions have actually lessened during the past two decades because of an "increased social mobility" (QA, 48). The acute aspect of the social question now is the problem of the adjustment of social progress to keep pace with the developments, scientific and technological, in production and in communication, which have so increased the efficiency of the economic order. It is the problem of the adjustment of social conditions so that all may participate; the correction of imbalances that exist between different sectors of national economies, between agriculture and industry, and between developed and underdeveloped nations.

It is in this context that the encyclical develops the principles of subsidiary aid to be given by public authority to the agricultural sector of the economy and to the depressed areas, and of the duty of international aid— emergency aid and long-range programs, financial and technical—which rests on the economically advanced nations in view of the solidarity of all men in the human family. There can be no indifference in this matter. "We are all equally responsible for the undernourished people" (MM, 158).

Two years after *Mater et Magistra* John XXIII issued the encyclical *Pacem in Terris*. This proved to be perhaps the most widely acclaimed social document of the Church in the modern world. In a sense *Pacem in Terris* is a summary of the social teaching of the preceding social encyclicals. Yet it is not a mere repetition. It unifies that teaching in the notion of the dignity of the human person, a notion which careful reading of the other encyclicals shows to be their pervading premise. The emphatic explication of this notion and its economic, social, and political corollaries in *Pacem in Terris* serve as a basis for its *aggiornamento* of Catholic social teaching.

The particular problem faced by *Pacem in Terris* is "the consolidation of peace in the world." It develops the theme mentioned in *Mater et Magistra:* the interdependence of people is growing, yet men are unable to achieve cooperation because of the absence of mutual trust which comes from failure to acknowledge principles of true order. *Pacem in Terris* makes the root of this true order respect for the dignity of the human person. The phrase "the dignity of the human person," or its equivalent, appears at least twenty-five times in the course of the encyclical as the ordering principle of the relations between individuals, between citizens and the public authority, between states, and between political communities and the world community.

The order of peace which emerges from this personal dignity is to be "an order founded on trust, built according to justice, vivified and integrated by charity, and put into practice in freedom" (PT, 167). All these elements of order are part of the traditional teaching of the Church on the subject. But in view of the rampant forces in the world today which would base human order on coercion, *Pacem in Terris* gives a new and special emphasis to the consideration of freedom: freedom in worship, freedom of association, freedom to choose rulers and government, participation in government, constitutional government, freedom of states in international affairs, international authority set up not by force but by common consent.

The principal thrust of *Pacem in Terris* is on this front of international order. Peace in the world is a consummation to which the lesser orders—between persons, between citizen and state, between states themselves—are integrating contributors, but which cannot be attained without a world-wide organization endowed with effective authority. The common good is taking on a new meaning in the historical evolution of the human family—the *universal* common good. And to provide for this common good the present means of normal diplomatic channels, of top level meetings or juridical instruments such as conventions and treaties, are inadequate.

To say that there is a world of difference between *Rerum Novarum* and *Pacem in Terris* is not an overstatement. Leo XIII was concerned with the protection of the depressed individual worker in a subhuman economic system; John XXIII stresses the need of international organization as a moral imperative of the social order.

Yet it should be emphasized that this is a growth in doctrine, not a change. It is an evolution, an unfolding, that finds new responses to ever newly emerging social problems. Throughout the encyclicals there is a continuous evolution of the fundamental principle that the goods of the earth should serve the use of all men according to the norms of justice and charity. Throughout them, too, the ever recurring measure of true social order is the dignity of the human person, whether it be on the level of the individual workers, who are not to be treated as mere chattels because "justice demands that the dignity of human personality be respected in them" (RN, 31), or on the level of the world community, which "must have as its fundamental objective the recognition, respect, safeguarding, and promotion of the rights of the human person" (PT, 139).

This is the dynamic character of natural law doctrine, so often misunderstood, which Pius XII pointed out in an address to the Italian Center of Studies for International

Reconciliation. Changes of economic, social, and political conditions demand new specifications of the natural law. But amid these changes the fundamental exigencies of human nature perdure and are transmitted from generation to generation.

CHAPTER TWO

THE COMMUNITY OF GOODS

At the heart of the social question is the problem of the ownership and use of material goods. This is clear enough from the earlier encyclicals which limit the question rather definitely to the consideration of the economic order, the relationship between capital and labor, between rich and poor, and between economic classes. It is clear, too, from the explanation of the term "the social question" given by Pius XII (see above, p. 19).

Such a limitation is not exclusive in the sense that the encyclicals treat no other phase of social life. *Rerum Novarum* and *Quadragesimo Anno* both devote considerable space to political philosophy, to the structure of the state, to the purpose and extent of civil authority, and to the need of social legislation. And necessarily so, because the solution of the social question even in this limited aspect profoundly affects the common good of the whole of society. In these encyclicals, however, the controlling consideration is concern for the economic condition of the workers.

When we come to the encyclicals of Pope John XXIII,

it seems that the comprehension of the social question has
been widened. In the economic field it is no longer merely
a question of the betterment of the workers individually
or as a class, but of the balancing of whole sectors of the
economy in their participation in the benefits of the social
progress, and of the relations between those nations which
enjoy a high standard of living and those which suffer
extreme poverty (MM, 122). Furthermore, there is an extension of the notion beyond the economic order, explicitly including those social and political rights that had
always been latent in the social question, but whose assertion, to be meaningful, presupposed a certain economic
foundation. To quote the encyclical *Pacem in Terris:*

> First of all, we note that the working classes have gradually
> gained ground in economic and public affairs. They began
> by claiming their rights in the socio-economic sphere. They
> extended their action then to claims on the political level.
> And, finally, they applied themselves to the acquisition of
> the benefits of a more refined culture. Today, therefore,
> workers all over the world bluntly refuse ever to be treated
> as if they were irrational objects without freedom, to be used
> at the arbitrary disposition of others. They insist that they
> be regarded as men with a share in every sector of human
> society: in the socio-economic sphere and in public life and
> in the fields of learning and culture (PT, 40).

In the progressive development of encyclical doctrine,
the "social question" thus must be understood today as the
problem of the economically depressed and their share
in the political, civil, and cultural benefits of society. Even
in this broadened meaning the social question still involves
the question of property. It still is concerned with the
economically depressed, and at its heart there still stands
the problem of the ownership and use of material goods.

This is clearly a proposition of *Mater et Magistra* and *Pacem in Terris* as well as of Vatican Council II. The latter calls private ownership or some other kind of dominion over material goods "a kind of prerequisite for civil liberties."[1] *Mater et Magistra* declares that the right to use the goods of the earth, to which corresponds the fundamental obligation of granting private property to all as far as possible, is ordinarily demanded as "a natural basis for living" (MM, 114). On the international level, "given the growing interdependence among nations, it is impossible to preserve a lasting and beneficial peace while glaring socio-economic inequalities persist" (MM, 157). *Pacem in Terris* describes the right to private property as "a suitable means for safe-guarding the dignity of the human person and for the exercise of responsibility in all fields" (PT, 21).

This is not an acceptance of Marxian economic deter-minism. Marx misread history in his Hegelian inspired effort to force all history into a predetermined mold. He contributed much to the social sciences by underlining the influence of economic development on social relationships. His condemnation of the inhumanity of *laissez-faire* capital-ism was a service to mankind. The same condemnation is found in language equally as strong in the social encyclicals. But Marx's attempt to read universal laws of history into the economic class conflict of his day, and to reduce all social, political, and intellectual processes of life to the mode of economic production was unrealistic philosophizing—the very thing for which he scorned idealism.

The centrality of the property question is sociological rather than philosophical. As St. Thomas pointed out long ago, a sufficiency of material goods is the condition on which a truly human life depends.[2]

This conditioning influence of poverty or affluence is plain to see. Adequate or inadequate housing and neighborhood environment, with their effect on family life and delinquency, hinge in great part on economic factors. The poor—the slum dwellers, ghetto dwellers—are also those who are inadequately protected in the exercise of civil rights and disadvantaged in cultural opportunities. The radical issue of the civil rights movement is that of economic discrimination against the Negro. Privacy and freedom often suffer in the instance of those who must depend on public welfare.

The teaching of the encyclicals on ownership and the use of property is in itself clear and unmistakable. It is, nevertheless, open to misinterpretation and misunderstanding especially on the part of those (even Catholics) whose concept of ownership is formed or colored by the popularized error of a complete consensus in the Western world on the meaning of the right of private property.

The opposition of the social teaching of the Church to communism is evident to all, but the mistake may be made of identifying the Catholic position with any system defending the right of private ownership. Many lump together in one group all who defend the right of private property. The result is that the Catholic position is identified in the minds of many with that of historical capitalism. The Church is put on the side of the wealthy as against the poor, an effect which the Communists themselves would desire.

Actually there are two opposed errors in this regard. There are two extremes: collectivism, which would abolish private ownership wholly or in part; and liberalism which defends an unrestricted right of ownership. (We use the term "liberalism" in the older sense in which it was used by *Quadragesimo Anno*. Today, because of the completely changed meaning of the term, we should be more correct in calling it individualism.) Both are opposed to Catholic social teaching, not only in the matter of property, which is but a focal point of opposition, but as complete philosophies of life.

Communism and liberalism are opposed to each other in the matter of property. But the opposition between them as philosophies of life is more apparent than real. Both start with one principle: the equality of all men. Both interpret that principle wrongly. To liberalism the equality of all men means the equal opportunity of every individual to get ahead, to advance himself by competition. The social nature of man with its consequent obligation to cooperate for the common good of all is neglected. To communism the equality of all men means the reduction of all to a common level of insignificance in the social community. The very real individual differences between men by reason of which they cannot be treated equally is ignored. Both interpretations are founded on a common error: materialism, blatant in one case, implicit in the other.

Liberalism or individualism, the philosophic heritage of America, developed chiefly in the seventeenth and eighteenth centuries. Its central doctrine, as its name implies, was that of individual freedom, individual liberty, the absolute independence of the individual of any authority which does not originate in himself. In this complete autonomy was to be found the true dignity of the individual man. It assumed different forms as it emphasized different kinds of freedom: religious, political, or economic.

Economic liberalism, which concerns us here, originated with the Physiocrats in France, whose doctrine, with certain modifications, was adopted by Adam Smith and became the matrix of the school of classical economists.[3] It may be characterized as a doctrine of the separation of the laws of life. Man is subject to laws in all spheres of life, religious, political, moral, and economic. But these spheres and laws are independent one from another; one must not interfere with another. The economic order has its own "economic laws" which are to be rigidly followed. It is governed by mechanically effective "natural laws" on the model of those which govern the physical universe. In this order man is called the "economic man"—a kind of puppet who always follows the motive of self-interest and always seeks his own profit. If he is allowed to follow this self-interest without impediment, the economic laws bring about a harmony between that interest and the common good. There is an "invisible hand" which better directs the economy than any human planning.[4]

There must be, therefore, no interference with these laws. There must be no regulation. Government has but one function here: to assure complete freedom of enterprise.[5] Absolutely free competition and freedom of contract are the necessary means for the proper working of the economic order. Beyond this: *laissez-faire*, *laissez-passer*. As far as private ownership is concerned: it is necessary for free competition. Every man must have a completely free disposition of his property. It is a right to acquire and acquire. Everyone is to look out for himself; there must be no restrictions on the use of property.

The application of these principles to industrial capitalism led inevitably to a concentration of wealth in the hands of a few. It led to the formation of social classes and of a depressed proletariat. It resulted in economic oppression: a denial in fact of economic freedom, a false freedom of contract. For there is no economic freedom when one or a few men hold all the means of production and the worker must accept the terms of employment that are imposed on him or starve.

Communism emerged as a reaction to the evils of liberalism. It saw the root of the inhuman condition of economic society in private property. Its remedy was to do away with the inequitable distribution of material goods by digging out this root. Henceforth the state would own all productive property. No man would any longer have power over another by reason of private ownership.[6] Communism appeared as a crusade for mankind. It had a Messianic character, promising man emancipation from all that is non-human or inhuman.

The deceptive nature of this promise, which many still fail to see, appears when this elimination of private ownership is seen in the whole context of Communist philosophy. For the denial of the right of property is but one part of a whole philosophy of man proposed and propagated by Marx and Engels.

According to the Marxian explanation, all reality—nature—is sensibly perceived matter which is continually evolving by a dialectic process. Nothing is static. There is a continuity between man and this nature, man being a product of matter, and the history of mankind being the highest phase of the evolution of matter.[7]

Man, moreover, is essentially a productive being; labor is his essential activity as well as the creative force of human values.[8] Economic production is therefore the ultimate source of the dynamism of history; and the basic determinant of the evolution of history is the economic mode of production.[9] All other institutions of human history—cultural, legal, political, religious—are but the super-structure, reflecting the prevailing method of economic production, and changing as the developing material forces of production come into conflict with existing property relations.[10] This economic determinism is driving mankind through the dialectic of class warfare to the realization of the perfect human reality, the Communist society, in which human labor and productive power, now completely co-operative and social, reach their ultimate perfection.[11]

Hence the social whole becomes the reality to whose evolution all else is subordinated. It is the perfect being. It alone has absolute value. The individual man is important only as a part.

Communism, therefore, as regards the right of private ownership, is at the opposite extreme from liberalism. It is a reaction to the evils that liberalism lets loose. But, as has been said, the opposition between these two systems as philosophies of life is more apparent than real. As a matter of fact, the principles of liberalism, logically pursued, lead to communism.[12] Liberalism has been called a half-way house on the road to communism.

As indicated before, both systems start with a common principle, the equality of all men, which they both interpret wrongly because of a common initial error, namely, materialism—the neglect or denial of the spiritual. Liberalism proposed for man the ideal of material prosperity and the satisfaction of material wants. Communism accepted this ideal but extended it to all rather than to a few powerful rich. Liberalism broke the link between the spiritual, moral realm and economics. Nothing must impede the operation of economic laws. Communism goes to the logical conclusion of eliminating the ineffectual spiritual and moral spheres as meaningless. The last obstacle to the operation of economic laws is the free individual. Thus liberalism supplied the intellectual climate in which communism could thrive and occasioned the crisis out of which it grew.

This materialism is the basic reason for the intransigent opposition of Catholic social teaching to both liberalism and communism. And the key to an understanding of the social teaching of the encyclicals on the right of ownership, as in the case of all rights, is the notion of the dignity of the human person. Every human being is a person, that is, his nature is endowed with intelligence and free will. Man is a creature of God; but he is a creature of special dignity, made in the image of God, spiritual and immortal, whose destiny is a possession of God forever. He may never, therefore, be "used"; he may never be a mere means for any other creature, either individual or collective. Catholic teaching, too, admits the principle of the equality of all men, but it is an equality in this human dignity, a dignity that forbids the slavery of some, as in individualism, or the slavery of all, as in communism.

Because of this dignity and destiny the natural law gives the human person certain inviolable rights (PT, 9). They are not derived from any human source but from the law of his very being which is a participation in the eternal law. They are beyond the destructive power of man and society. They are "universal, inviolable and inalienable." Among these rights is the right to private property.

All the social encyclicals are forceful in their affirmation of this right; but against the excesses of individualism they are equally strong in stressing the limits of the right. These limits spring from the twofold aspect of private property, individual and social. The right of property and also its limitations are derived from one fundamental principle: the purpose of material goods, which is to serve the use of all men as human persons (QA, 45). Property, therefore, is not an end in itself. It is but a means so that goods may serve the use of all men in a way which is in conformity with their dignity as human persons. If it interferes with that end, if it ceases to be a means, it loses its justification in natural law.

The right of ownership, consequently, is not unlimited. With ownership there comes the duty of using one's goods to serve the common good. There comes the duty of the stewardship of wealth, a duty which according to an analysis of the encyclical *Quadragesimo Anno*, would seem to be the principal duty of social justice.[13]

The evolution of encyclical teaching on the matter of ownership concerns principally this duty of stewardship, that is, the social obligations attached to property. This does not, however, mean that these obligations have been realized only since the publication of *Rerum Novarum*. The social function of property is a "doctrinal point constantly set forth by our predecessors" as John XXIII points out in *Mater et Magistra* (MM, 119). It is a part of the tradition of Catholic social teaching that goes back to the earliest history of Christianity. Rather, this development is one of clarification and emphasis according to the needs of the times. Vatican Council II summarized the need for this emphasis: "Profound and rapid changes make it particularly urgent that no one, ignoring the trend of events or drugged by laziness, content himself with a merely individualistic morality."[14]

Leo XIII was confronted by the fallacious remedy for the plight of the dehumanized worker which socialism offered: "that it is necessary to do away with private possession of goods and in its place to make the goods of individuals common to all, and that the men who preside over a municipality or who direct the entire State should act as administrators of these goods" (RN, 7). Consequently he was concerned in establishing as the basic principle in seeking help for the masses "that private ownership must be preserved inviolate."

In this context, *Rerum Novarum* devotes much more space than any of the succeeding encyclicals to an explanation of the traditional arguments for the right of private property, from a consideration of the self-provident nature of man, from the needs of family life, and from its effect on public peace and prosperity (RN, 11–12, 19–20, 65–66). The social aspect of this right is by no means neglected. The "common use" doctrine of St. Thomas is cited and briefly explained; the duties of the rich are detailed; and finally Pope Leo sums up his teaching in words which would be repeated years afterward in *Mater et Magistra:* "Whoever has received from the bounty of God a greater share of goods whether corporeal and external, or of the soul, has received them for this purpose, namely, that he employ them for his own perfection and likewise, as a servant of Divine Providence, for the benefit of others" (RN, 31–37).

Perhaps it was because of Leo's insistence on the inviolability of the right of property against the Socialists of his time that his teaching was misunderstood. At any rate, forty years later, at the time of the writing of *Quadragesimo Anno*, Pius XI felt it necessary to defend the doctrine of his predecessor against the calumny that Leo had taken the part of the rich against the non-owning worker (QA, 44). Accordingly, the burden of his teaching on the subject is to explain

what has always been "unanimously maintained" by the
Church: that ownership has a twofold character called
individual or social as it regards either separate persons or
the common good.

There is no need to expound again the arguments for
the existence of the right itself which Pope Leo so "strongly
defended." The need is to insist that the root of this right
also produces grave social obligations. That root is the
divinely ordered purpose of the goods of the earth: the
service and use of all men. "Nature, rather the Creator
himself, has given man the right of private ownership not
only that individuals may be able to provide for themselves
and their families but also that the goods which the Creator
destined for the entire family of mankind may through this
institution truly serve this purpose" (QA, 45). And again:
"The division of goods which results from private ownership was established by nature itself in order that created
things may serve the needs of mankind in a fixed and stable
order" (QA, 56).

Several conclusions are drawn from this essential social
aspect of ownership. First, regulation of property rights in
view of the situational requirements of the common good
is a proper function of public authority—it is not socialism.
Second, the increase in riches which results from economic
development must be shared proportionately by both capital
and labor; the common good, not profit or what the market
will bear to the advantage of either side, is the just norm
of this sharing. And finally there is the grave precept which
rests on the rich of using their superfluous income, that is,
income which a person "does not need to sustain life fittingly
and with dignity" (echoing the words of *Rerum Novarum*) for
the benefit of others (QA, 50).

This last obligation does not imply that the rich must give away their wealth. The proper use of wealth does not entail a utopian distribution. It is a stewardship, which connotes intelligence, prudence, and responsibility. Almsgiving may be a use of superfluous income dictated by the urgency of an individual situation. But dependence on a dole should not be the chronic condition of the poor. Their human dignity and the good of society demand that they should be put in a position of being able to provide for themselves. Therefore, a fulfillment of the stewardship of wealth, singled out as "particularly suited to the needs of the times," is the investment of larger incomes so that opportunity for gainful work may be abundant (QA, 51).

The insistence on the social aspect of property could hardly be more forceful or unmistakable than that in *Quadragesimo Anno;* yet when we come to *Mater et Magistra* we find added emphasis on this same point. Pope John's explanation of the matter is not, as some have said, merely a reiteration of traditional teaching. It shows a nuance of treatment and expression which climaxes that tradition and gives an inspiring insight into the meaning of his predecessors. He makes it clear that, in Catholic social teaching, the right of private ownership is unintelligible without its social aspect. Social duties are not merely connected with ownership but they are "intrinsic" to it. "The social function of property derives its validity from the very nature of the right of ownership" (MM, 119–120). The substance of this statement is not different from that of *Quadragesimo Anno*, but its happy formulation is geared to meet a new problem.

The changes of the past decade, of which Pope John continually speaks, did give rise to new questions, and in

answering them the Pope uncovered new facets of the traditional teaching. These questions pertained both to the
existence of the right of property itself and to the social
aspect of property.

There is first of all the problem of the very relevance of
the right of private ownership in the modern world. Several
socio-economic considerations contribute to spreading a
doubt whether the right of private ownership, including
ownership of productive goods, has lost its importance in
the present state of affairs. For instance, the increasingly
pronounced separation of ownership and control in larger
economic units and the anonymity ot the corporate structure seem to have weakened a fundamental argument for the
need of private ownership, namely, responsibility in the
management of property.[15] Ownership is necessary so
that there may be a conscientious direction of material goods
to the end intended by God. The owner is the responsible
steward.

The modern separation of ownership and management
does create problems of control, as anti-trust legislation,
price fixing, and conspiracy scandals make abundantly clear.
But they are problems which arise from bigness, a necessary
characteristic of any large industrialized society, rather than
from private ownership. Nor are they solved by the elimination of private ownership. As the encyclical points out, these
problems "arise regardless of whether the capital that makes
possible these vast undertakings belongs to private citizens
or to public agencies" (MM, 104). And the implication
which can be gathered from the encyclical's repeated invoca-
tion of the principle of subsidiarity is that these problems
would be exacerbated by the public ownership of all
economic giants.

Again, given modern insurance systems and social security programs, the need of private ownership to make provision for the future has definitely diminished. Whereas formerly security in life depended on property ownership, now various social welfare institutions allow a great many to "face the future with serenity" without the ownership of properties (MM, 105).

The insight of Pope John's reply to this objection should not be overlooked. It exhibits the full humanism of the natural law doctrine of private ownership. Material security in life is not its only function. Human existence is. And this human existence includes freedom. Security may have been the principal value of property in an earlier, less socialized time, but today, while the consideration of security retains a true validity, the protection of human freedom and dignity comes to the fore as its radical benefit. Society or the state might possibly be a provider of material sufficiency for all citizens. But it could do the same thing for a herd of animals. And in the difference between animal life and human life lies the necessity of private ownership. "The exercise of freedom finds both a guarantee and an incentive in the right of ownership" (MM, 109). Whatever modern social welfare provisions may be, therefore, the right of private property must be maintained as "both the guarantee of the essential freedom of the individual and an indispensable element in the structuring of a sound social order" (MM, 111).

Finally, the fact is alleged as an objection "that today men strive to acquire professional skills rather than to become owners of property." Work and rights founded on work are sought rather than capital, as sources of income. The importance of capital ownership increasingly dwindles (MM, 106).

Here, in answer, *Mater et Magistra* definitely enlarges the notion of ownership. Times have changed and forms of ownership change with them. The concept of ownership as possession of a small farm, some livestock, and a neat frame house is perhaps an ideal for a civilization predominantly rural. But with an ever growing urbanization of life, ownership, as a means for safeguarding the dignity of the human person and for the exercise of responsibility in all fields, must include not merely material goods but also what Vatican Council II calls "intangible goods."[16] Professional skills, professional practices, job security must be classified as such intangibles, and for most city dwellers today they replace the more romantic property symbols of a simpler society.

Pope John views this change without nostalgia. He does not indeed, disparage the ideal of family type farms, but highly praises and encourages it (MM, 142–149). But, realist that he is, he recognizes the modern trend and welcomes it, where it applies, as elevating work, the immediate product of the human person, above capital which is merely an instrument. "Such a view of work," he declares, "may no doubt be considered a step forward in the process of human civilization" (MM, 107).

Despite these objections, therefore, "the right of private ownership of goods, including productive goods, has a permanent validity" (MM, 109).

The second question which modern social changes bring up concerns the social function of property today. In a way this is the inverse side of the problem mentioned above of the increased welfare functions of the state. Public agencies now increasingly care for the poor, the aged, the sick, the unemployed, and the handicapped. Does this mean

for the wealthy that the social function of private ownership has today become obsolete? After all, the revenue
which finances the various welfare programs comes from the
taxes that property holders pay. Perhaps, then, in modern
society the social duties of wealth are fulfilled, though
indirectly, through the paying of taxes.

This is the question which Pope John answers in the
negative, adding the trenchant proposition: "The social function of property derives its validity from the very nature of
the right of ownership." Although the state may further
extend its activity in the field of social welfare, the nature of
private ownership remains unchanged. It remains intrinsi-
cally social, never shedding its relations to the benefit of
others and to the common good (MM, 120).

Obviously, as the encyclical points out, there always
remained urgent "tragic situations and needs" which public
agencies cannot assist. Obviously, too, the more personal
assistance given by individuals or civic groups is of its nature
more apt to respect the spiritual values proper to human
dignity, than are the impersonal agencies of the state. To all
of which must be added the modern perduring obligation
of the rich, which *Quadragesimo Anno* indicated, of socially
beneficial investment of wealth. Despite social changes,
therefore, the social function of property remains today both
theoretically valid and practically urgent.

With regard to this social use of wealth, Vatican Council
II, which presents a concise summary of the social encyclicals, uses an expression which calls for some explanation.
"The fathers and doctors of the Church held this view, teaching that men are obliged to come to the relief of the poor,
and to do so not merely out of their superfluous goods."[17]

This statement seems to contradict traditional teaching,

according to which the obligation of helping the poor is dependent precisely on the possession of superfluous goods. Thus *Rerum Novarum:* "No one, certainly, is obliged to assist others out of what is required for his own necessary use or that of his family, or even to give to others what he himself needs to maintain his station in life becomingly and decently . . . but when the demands of necessity and propriety have been sufficiently met, it is a duty to give to the poor out of that which remains" (RN, 36). Again in *Quadragesimo Anno:* "Furthermore, a person's superfluous income, that is, income which he does not need to sustain life fittingly and with dignity, is not left wholly to his own free determination. Rather the Sacred Scriptures and the Fathers of the Church constantly declare in the most explicit language that the rich are bound by a very grave precept to practice alms-giving, beneficence and munificence"(QA, 50).

The apparent contradiction is perhaps explained by recalling a distinction, which is indicated in the encyclicals and has always been a part of Catholic moral teaching, between goods that are "superfluous" to the absolute needs of the owner, but which would be "necessary" for the maintenance of a certain standard of living, which varies with different social classes. To this distinction of superfluities there corresponds a distinction of "necessary goods": those which are necessary for the preservation of human life ("absolute necessities") and those which are necessary for one's social position ("conventional necessities"). As is evident, goods which are "necessary" in this second sense are "superfluous" if looked at from the viewpoint of what is needed to maintain the human life of an owner and his dependents.

It would seem that Vatican Council II had this in mind

when it extended the obligation beyond superfluous goods. There is no obligation of using the "absolute necessities" of life for others (although such sacrifice in the case of an owner with no dependents may be supreme charity); but the obligation does extend to "conventional necessities." These seem to be the "superfluous goods" to which the Council refers, as appears from an examination of the references to the teaching of the Fathers and Doctors of the Church given by the Council.

Basil, for instance,[18] in the homily which is cited by the Council, speaks of the evil of avarice, and, in vivid patristic imagery, compares the avaricious man with a glutton who would rather burst than give his leftovers to the needy. Gregory[19] teaches that we should give the neighbor even things that are necessary, such as food and clothing; but he adds that the precept bears on a man who has an extra tunic, not merely one (*quia hoc de uno dici nequit*). Bonaventure,[20] treating of almsgiving, indicates the two kinds of necessary goods we have mentioned, absolute necessities (*secundum arctitudinem vitae*) and conventional necessities (*secundum communem modum vivendi*), and restricts the obligation to the second category.

The expression of the Council does not deny or contradict traditional explanations of the obligations of property owners. It merely serves to underscore, for the modern world in which a certain Hedonism has blurred the distinction between what is necessary and what is superfluous, how foreign any individualistic mentality is to the Church's doctrine of ownership.

CHAPTER THREE

THE SOCIAL COMMUNITY

At the close of the last century, social organization, outside of the remote political apparatus of the civil government, was a privilege of the elite. What there was of it was synonymous with "high society," business men's clubs, and tightly closed circles of patrons of the arts. There were, of course, religiously inspired societies and fraternities motivated by a true social-mindedness; but these were comparatively few and directed principally to the alleviation which their charity could bring to the suffering of injustice rather than to the correction of the injustice itself. For the most part, "social endeavor" was a condescending gesture towards the unfortunate, best illustrated by the Thanksgiving or Christmas baskets which the wife of the factory owner distributed in season to hired hands and their families.

This veneer of sociability scarcely cloaked the prevalent individualism. Attitudes and values were colored by that social Darwinism which saw life as a competitive struggle of individuals in which the fittest survived. This was a reassuring philosophy for those on the top, but it was an invitation to hopelessness for the poor. They were free to compete like anyone else, but "on their own" as individuals. And the successful heroes of Horatio Alger depended as much on luck as they did on industrious virtue.

Labor organization and unionism for mutual help, which we take so much for granted today, and which Leo XIII defended as natural rights, were barely tolerated legally, were socially discredited and economically resisted. Early attempts to organize were squelched as criminal conspiracies; and even after the doctrine of conspiracy was abandoned about the middle of the 19th century, the courts still sided with employers in crippling union organization and activity. It was not until 1935 that the right of labor to form unions of its own choosing and to bargain collectively was given legal federal guarantee in the United States.

The seventy years which intervened between Leo XIII and John XXIII, and especially the last thirty years, have seen a complete reversal of this situation. In 1961 *Mater et Magistra* could state: "one of the characteristic features of our epoch is socialization" (MM, 59).

Socialization as understood and explained in the encyclical has nothing to do with socialism. It simply means group activity. It is "the growing interdependence of men in society giving rise to various patterns of group life and activity and in many instances to social institutions established on a juridical basis" (MM, 59).

The institutions in which socialization expresses itself are both private and public. Blue Cross and Blue Shield, educational associations, parent-teacher organizations, trade unions, credit unions, cooperatives, and even the Little Leagues are instances of the former; the latter is evident in such things as social security, public employment agencies, medicare, state aid to education, subsidization of agriculture or industry, the TVA, the anti-poverty program and the Peace Corps.

Internal and external factors have contributed to this socializing trend. "Technical and scientific progress, greater productive efficiency and a higher standard of living" are indicated by *Mater et Magistra* as some of these factors. Big business, whose spokesmen sometimes express fear of its impact on the future of free enterprise, has itself had no small share in its growth. Men have become necessarily more interdependent in the mass movement and activity that have accompanied the modern urbanization and mechanization of life. At the same time, fundamental human needs for fellowship and love have often been thwarted by our growing industrial system and denied by the selfish individualism of some of the system's leaders. Externally, the movements (not the philosophy) of communism and socialism, with their promise of peace, plenty, and security, have been a strong influence which has forced the Western world to reconsider its social structure and to listen to the legitimate claims of those to whom that promise appeals.

It is true that this socialization is not without danger, because, as *Mater et Magistra* warns, it touches the deepest concerns of the human person. The encyclical is quite frank in indicating these dangers which it reduces to a sub-mergence of personal dignity and a shrugging off of responsibility.

> Socialization multiplies institutional structures and extends more and more to minute details the juridical control of human relations in every walk of life. As a consequence, it restricts the range of an individual's freedom of action. It uses means, follows methods and creates an atmosphere

which make it difficult for one to reach judgements free from
external pressures, to work on his own initiative, to exercise
responsibility and to assert and enrich his personality
(MM, 62).

There is the danger, too, of an unsound view of the
common good on the part of public officials, of the sup-
pression of the "effective autonomy" of social groups within
the state, and of the failure of these groups themselves to
treat their members as persons encouraged to take a part
in the community's affairs (MM, 65).

More popularly, fears are expressed of "creeping
socialism" and of the advent of the welfare state and totalitarianism. And there are those who would exploit the growing socialization with this in view. For them socialization is a
product of natural forces working in a deterministic way.

If these dangers, however, are avoided—and they can
be, according to Pope John, since socialization is "a creation
of free men" and not the result of social determinism—
socialization carries advantages by reason of which "it
offers hope of promoting in individuals the expression and
development of their personal characteristics" and "results
in an organic reconstruction of society . . . as the indispensable prerequisite for satisfying abundantly the demands of
social justice" (MM, 67).

[Socialization] makes possible the satisfaction of many
personal rights, especially those of a soci-economic nature.
The right to the indispensable means of human subsistence,
to health services, to instruction at a higher level, to more
thorough professional formation, to housing, to employment, to suitable leisure and to decent recreation are typical
examples. In addition, through increasing systematization
of modern media of mass communications—press, motion
pictures, radio, television—it becomes possible for individ-

uals to participate, as it were, in human events even on a worldwide scope (MM, 61).

Socialization, therefore, despite its perils, is according to *Mater et Magistra* "also the fruit and expression of a natural tendency almost irrepressible in human beings—the tendency to unite for the purpose of obtaining objectives which each ambitions but which are beyond the capacity of individuals" (MM, 60).

Hence, the danger to be feared is not so much an increase in the socialization of life. Man is meant to live in community. He is by nature social. Group life and group activity are "the fruit and expression of a natural tendency." But the natural sociability of man is not always understood even by those who mouth the phrase. Often, in fact, the arguments for the natural sociability of man are so presented as to support the individualist thesis. Man is thus presented as a being who finds in society a remedy for the defects of his nature. Society appears as a necessary evil—a sort of afterthought in the constitution of man—under which he accepts a limitation of his freedom in exchange for the supplementation of his natural deficiency.

There is no doubt that the deficiencies of solitary existence are a sign of the need of social life. Leo XIII's expression of this fact is familiar:

> Man's natural instinct moves him to live in civil society, for he cannot, if dwelling apart, provide himself with the necessary requirements of life nor procure the means of developing his mental and moral faculties. Hence, it is divinely ordained that he should lead his life—be it family, social or civil—with his fellowmen, amongst whom alone his several wants can be adequately supplied.[1]

But social life is not founded solely or even primarily

on individual "wants"—wants in a strictly utilitarian sense. Any material creature has like needs. A plant needs soil, moisture, and sun, and irrational animals "depend" on other animals for birth, for food. But none of these "needs" make such beings social. Irrational animals use other creatures according to necessary instincts, but they cannot cooperate for a common end, they cannot knowingly and freely cooperate for a common purpose, because they cannot reason.

Here is indicated the true root of sociability: rationality. Because man is rational he can love and communicate goodness to others; in this ability there is reflected in the human person the image of God who is love and who creates only to communicate His goodness. This potentiality of human nature is brought to realization in society. "It is society which affords the opportunities for the development of all the individual and social gifts bestowed on human nature. These natural gifts have a value surpassing the immediate interests of the moment, for in society they reflect the divine perfection which would not be true were man to live alone."[2]

Again, it is through reason that mankind adapts all creation to its service, thus bringing creation to its teleological perfection. Such complete adaptation, however, is the work not of one man or of one human intellect but of all, each contributing his part, the findings and accomplishments of one generation being passed on to the next, conserved and improved through social institutions.

> Human society . . . ought to be regarded above all as a spiritual reality; one in which men communicate knowledge to each other in the light of truth; in which they can enjoy their rights and fulfill their duties, and are inspired to strive for goods of the spirit. Society should enable men to share in and enjoy every legitimate expression of beauty. It should

encourage them constantly to pass on to others all that is best in themselves, while they strive to make their own the spiritual achievements of others. These are the values which continually give life and basic orientation to cultural expressions, economic and social institutions, political movements and forms, laws and all other structures by which society is outwardly established and constantly developed (PT, 36).

Society, therefore, exists for the more perfect realization of the perfection of man as a person. Therein his rational life comes to fulfillment in mutual communication of goods. It is not, therefore, a remedy for the defects of nature which is sought in society but rather the more perfect expression and fulfillment of personality. Man is not social because he needs the aid of others, but conversely, as St. Thomas expresses it, because he is naturally social he needs the help of others to come to his perfection.[3]

Men achieve their personal perfection according to the plan of God, not as isolated individuals but in mutual complementation and aid, the giving of which is, therefore, itself a part of that perfection. Life in society is not merely a utilitarian expedient; it is itself a moral good.

One of the best expressions of this essential sociability, so necessary for judging the phenomenon of socialization, was given by Vatican Council II: "By his innermost nature man is a social being, and unless he relates himself to others he can neither live nor develop his potential.[4]

The danger is rather in trying to fit the factual socialization of life into the individualistic scheme of society which is still widely accepted. The liberalism of the past two centuries has left this paradoxical heirloom.

Here again we meet the term, "liberalism"—one of the most confused and confusing terms of this day and age.[5] As it was used earlier in this work, the meaning of liberalism was clear enough. It designated the doctrine of classical economic liberalism, the individualistic system of *laissez-faire*. But, as noted, the meaning of the term has changed completely. Today it signifies the position of those who would extend the role of government in economic and social life—exactly the opposite of *laissez-faire*. And the defenders of the old liberalism are now Conservatives.

This complete reversal is not without its internal logic nor its practical import. For there are certain tenets of the old liberalism, which, as constant in its various sectarian forms,[6] explain its transformation, and which, as still prevalent, contribute to the feared perversion of modern socialization. These tenets are its concepts of society and authority.

Liberalism's concept of society is an embodiment of the political theory of Locke and Rousseau: an individualist contractualism. In this theory, man is by nature "in a state of perfect freedom" according to Locke;[7] and a "solitary" according to Rousseau.[8] He is a completely independent individual, who enjoys the "natural rights"[9] of life, liberty, and property. Sociability and individuality are not equally original in man's nature. The former is a derivative of the latter.

It is to protect their individual natural freedom that men freely form society by a compact, the one purpose of which is to realize the fullest freedom for each individual compatible with a like legal freedom for others.[10] Men are inclined to society as to an investment for individual self-interest. Society is a utilitarian expedient for the insurance of mutual freedom.

Because of this concept men have lost the idea of true community, of a true living together, of a social whole.

Society is a mere sum of individuals. The society of individualism is nothing distinct from the mere sum of the men who form it. Individual and society are concepts which differ quantitatively, society being a name to denote a number of self-sufficient individuals who have freely contracted to submit themselves to a common power, authority, for the purpose of assuring equality of individual opportunity. In so far as the formation of society results in any new being, it is the being of political institutions, of legislative bodies, courts and police forces, which concretize the political authority and constitute the "state."

Hence individualism tends to identify the social order with the political order, society with the state. Furthermore, since government is the agency through which the state acts, socialization necessarily implies government activity and control. Here, in the identification of social action with state action, lies the danger of totalitarianism and socialism, a danger that grows as long as the socialization of life is crowded into this liberalistic scheme.

This absorption of society in the state, according to *Mater et Magistra*, must be avoided if the negative consequences of socialization are to be avoided: "We consider it necessary that the intermediate groups and numerous social enterprises through which socialization tends to express itself should enjoy an effective autonomy" (MM, 65).

The same absorption was one of the principal complaints of Pius XI in *Quadragesimo Anno*. Speaking of the reformation of social institutions, he says that he has

> primarily the state in mind. This does not mean that all hope of salvation is to be placed in state intervention. We refer rather to the situation of fact resulting from the evil which we have called Individualism. We once had a prosper-

ous social system which owed its development to the wide
variety of associations organically linked together. That
structure has been overturned and all but demolished. Individuals are left practically alone with the state" (QA, 78).

And this false antithesis of individual and state has also
occasioned the complete reversal of the meaning of liberalism. Sectarian liberalism has always sought the freedom
of man. The dignity of man, as has been said, is conceived
as consisting in his independence of any authority or power
outside himself; and the various forms of sectarian liberalism are explained by the varying authorities or powers which
they have sought to eliminate in the interest of freedom.

Freedom is still the objective of the new liberalism.
Since the time of the industrial revolution, however, it has
been the growing power of big business and industry which
has threatened freedom: the freedom of the working masses.
As a result, because of the dichotomy which liberalism itself
introduced, this has meant reliance on the state. The working
class threatened with economic slavery (and the defenders
of the workers) had no one to turn to for an amelioration of
conditions except to the state. The consequence has been
the insistence of modern Liberals on an increase of state
power to regulate business and to legislate for welfare—
in the interest of freedom.

Interwoven with this individualistic image of society is
liberalism's explanation of authority. Liberalism admits
authority; not, however, as a divinely instituted right to
command, but as a contractually determined expedient for
the reconciliation of private interests. The weakness of
liberalism is that it looks upon authority as something
opposed to freedom, not as its complement. It is a restraint
on "natural" individual freedom, and in that sense it is an

evil. Authority is nevertheless a necessary evil because of the defects of man. Authority consists in the power which the contracting free individuals agree to give. It is something which, because of its human origin, is limited by human convention, not obectively determined in principle by the divinely instituted order of finality. There results in this concept an essential indetermination in authority that leaves it subject to the pressure of historical events.[11]

The danger that modern socialization flirts with, given this concept of authority, is evident. In the beginning the philosophy of individualism restricted state power to the role of an umpire securing equal freedom to competing individuals. Today, however, the old principle of "no intervention" has broken down. The state does in fact regulate business activities; it has assumed a welfare function, and is increasing that function. But—and here is the difficulty and the danger—a philosophy which holds such a principle evidently can supply no limit to intervention once it is admitted. The way is opened to the totalitarian state.

In this critical area of the relationship between liberty and authority, two basic propositions underlie the teaching of all the social encyclicals and are particularly in evidence in the development of *Pacem in Terris*. The first is that man is created in the image of God for the eternal possession of God; the second, that the existence of the state with real and effective authority is of divine institution.

From the first proposition we have the exalted dignity of the individual man as a person, by reason of which he can never be entirely subordinated to any human institution. Rational, free, and immortal, man is not the passive object of social life; he is its source and foundation (PT, 26). He is not the means of social life and prosperity; he is its end.

All human institutions, cultural, economic, political, have the perfection of the human person as their purpose.

From the second proposition, namely, that the existence of the state with real effective authority is of divine institution, we have the dignity of political authority in its participation in the authority of God. From the common foundation of both independent personality and political authority in the divinely established order of beings and purposes must ultimately come their reconciliation (PT, 47–51). It is the neglect of their common divine foundation that has led to the modern conflict between liberty and authority.

From what has been said it follows that society can never absorb or destroy the individual person. It is also clear, however, that not every sacrifice of an individual good is an invasion of personal liberty, which has as its purpose the self-realization of man within the order of his divinely given nature. Man, an intelligent responsible agent, must realize his personal perfection by his own initiative. But the same obligation which rests on him to seek that perfection also places on him the obligation of seeking those social ends which are the condition of his personal perfection.

It is, furthermore, natural that many relatively autonomous spheres of cooperation should grow from the social nature of man. For the ends which man seeks through society are themselves many and diverse. Some of these ends are directly ordained by nature, as, for instance, the propagation of the race and the education of children; others are freely chosen, such as those of cultural or professional associations. About each of these various ends different social groups arise, all springing from the rational nature of man seeking self-realization through cooperation, each with a responsibility for the attainment of its specific end and consequently, too, with the power of self-determination in pursuing that end.

The autonomy of these groups is real, derived as they are from the self-determining rational nature of man; but it is also, as we have mentioned, relative. For there is a further general common good which unites them all in a universal society—the civil society or state. That general common good consists in the opportunity for the full temporal complementation of the human person which results from the cooperation of these many qualitatively various groups.

The principle of social unity is, thus, not the external force of political government but rather the existence of a common good or of a number of related common goals towards which rational men freely move.

From this natural plurality of social ends, therefore, there results a natural plurality of communities linked in a supreme unity of order, the civil society; the functions, authority, and autonomy of each group being determined by its proper end.

Consequently, neither is the state synonymous with society, nor are the functions of the state coextensive with those of society. The necessity of attaining the common good of the social whole, being part of the divine plan for man, legitimizes state authority in principle, but it also, in principle, limits that authority. For the common good is also decisive of the rights and responsibilities of individual persons and social forms that grow from the rational nature of man within the state. State authority may only protect, assist, and coordinate the inferior social forms. It may not abolish them or substitute itself for them.

Hence is derived the principle of subsidiarity which

Pius XI calls "a fundamental principle of social philosophy unshaken and unchangeable":

> Just as it is wrong to withdraw from the individual and commit to a group what private enterprise and industry can accomplish, so too it is an injustice, a grave evil and a disturbance of right order for a larger and higher association to arrogate to itself functions which can be performed efficiently by smaller and lower societies.... The state therefore should leave to smaller groups the settlement of business of minor importance which otherwise would greatly distract it; it will thus carry out with greater freedom, power and success the task belonging to it alone because it alone can efficiently accomplish these: directing, watching, stimulating, restraining, as circumstances suggest and necessity demands (QA, 79–80).

Mater et Magistra and *Pacem in Terris* both reiterate this principle, stressing the fact that state activity, no matter what its breadth or depth may be, must always aim at effecting those social conditions which permit men to pursue more readily the integral development of their personalities (MM, 55; PT, 65–66). This is the common good, "the whole reason for the existence of civil authorities."

There is a distinction indicated here which recent sociological and philosophical writings formulate as the distinction between society and the state. The import of the distinction is this: the common good of politically organized society is effected socially, that is, through the well-ordered communication of all the members of the body politic, not exclusively politically, that is, not through the all-absorbing action of that part of civil society which is especially charged with the safeguarding of the common good, namely, the state and its agencies. Social activity is not, therefore, a synonym for state activity. All the social affairs of the members of civilized society have a political dependency, as the objects of the protection of public authority, and they all have a political repercussion, as contributing to the public welfare; but they are not on that account political affairs or activities.

How important this distinction looms is clear from what has been said about liberalism's confusion.

Although (as far as I know) the formula, "society is not the state," does not occur anywhere in the social encyclicals, the substance of this expression is verified in them all. It is a part of the Catholic social tradition. It comes as a surprise, therefore, to read Father John Courtney Murray's assertion that "Pope John . . . clearly accepts the distinction that seems to be missing from Leo XIII, namely, the distinction between society and the state."[12] This dismissal of the teaching of Leo XIII on the subject does not seem to be well considered.

Father Murray himself is very clear and emphatic in his proposition of this distinction. To avoid the errors consequent upon the identification of society and the state, he has worked out a set of concepts distinguishing "civil society," "political society," "state," "people," and "government."[13] Maritain, in his book, *Man and the State*, has proposed a similar set of concepts and terms. According to both, the term "state" does not signify a society at all.

Thus, according to Murray the state is something connoted by political society, which in turn is civil society as politically organized. "The state is not the body politic but that particular subsidiary functional organization of the body politic, whose special function regards the good of the whole . . . it is a set of institutions combined into a complex agency of social control and public service . . . its functions are not coextensive with the functions of society; they are limited by the fact that it is only one, although the highest subsidiary function of society."[14]

The formulation of Maritain is very similar. The state differs from the body politic (political society) as part from the whole. "The state is only that part of the body politic especially concerned with the maintenance of law, the promotion of the common welfare and public order . . . which specializes in the interest of the whole. The state is not a man or a body of men; it is a set of institutions combined into a top-most machine . . . superior to the other organs or collective parts of the body politic, but not superior to the body politic itself."[15]

These refinements afford a useful insight which clarifies and, in a way, simplifies a difficult problem. They are not, however, accepted by all. Woelfl, for instance, challenges them and rejects the validity of Murray's and Maritain's concept of the state.[16] More to the point for present purposes, these distinctions as such are not found in the social encyclicals.

Without a doubt the term "state" is ambiguous. It can be understood as the political community, the perfect society, the government, or the public agencies of government. The term is used in all these senses by the encyclicals. This can be verified in all the social encyclicals, but restricting consideration to *Pacem in Terris* alone, these diverse senses of the term "state" are evident. It is used as a synonym for the political community (PT, 86), where the equality of these communities is discussed; the "state" is called (quoting the words of Pius XII) a "necessary society" (PT, 47) which is included in the absolute order of beings; the "state" and government or its public agencies are understood as synonymous in the explanation of the principle of subsidiarity (PT, 65–66).

Despite this multiple meaning of the term, the particular significance it bears in different sections of the encyclicals is clarified by each context in which it is used. Clearly included among these encyclical usages is that proposed by Murray and Maritain as distinguishing society from state, according to which the state is "that part of the body politic which is especially concerned with the promotion of the common welfare," and that "set of institutions combined into a complex agency of social control and public service." However, it is also clear that acceptance of the distinction between society and state does not depend on their precise terminology.

The test of the distinction between society and the state, necessary for the exclusion of social monism or totalitarianism (and this seems to be the purport of the precisions made by both Maritain and Murray) is the principle of subsidiarity. According to this principle, as explained by *Quadragesimo Anno*, *Mater et Magistra*, and *Pacem in Terris*, the attainment of the common good is the social function of all individuals, groups, agencies, and associations who are members of the "state" understood as the politically organized society. On the other hand, the "state," taken in the sense of the agencies within the political unity which exercise supreme authority, has the political function of coordinating the lesser groups and supplementing their deficiencies—of furnishing help to the members of the social body, "directing, watching, urging, restraining as occasion demands and necessity requires" (QA, 79).

Put to this test, the encyclical *Rerum Novarum* comes off with full marks. Leo XIII did not enunciate the principle of

subsidiarity; this remained for Pius XI. But the introduction
to the formulation of the principle by Pope Pius is significant: he refers to the thought and care which Leo devoted
to the restoration of social order according to the principles
of sound philosophy (QA, 76), suggesting thus that his
formulation is a summary of Leo's teaching. This becomes
more than a suggestion when Pope Pius further roots his
idea of vocational groups, through which the principle of
subsidiarity will be made effective, in the "free associations"
so "clearly and lucidly explained by our predecessor"
(QA, 87).

Everything but the title, "Principle of Subsidiarity," is
contained in *Rerum Novarum*. The later encyclicals only name
the principle and develop its application to growing state
activity in view of the increasing complexity of the social
order.

Rerum Novarum's advocacy of the freedom and right of
citizens to form groups for the purpose of social cooperation
through which the good of civil society is achieved is a by-
word of Catholic social teaching. It is, according to the
encyclical, from the natural sociability of man that private
associations, for the purpose of carrying out business or
engaging in trade, arise within the state (of which they are,
as it were, so many parts [RN, 72]). Associations of workers,
or workers and employers together, are "formed by their
own right" (RN, 69), and enjoy an autonomy in the running
of their own affairs. They are themselves to regulate their
mutual relations and to settle disputes by their own rules
and boards of arbitration (RN, 78). Provision of employment and insurance against "sudden and unforeseen changes
in industry" as well as against illness and age are indicated
as the functions of these private associations (RN, 79).

Economic associations are the chief concern of *Rerum Novarum*, but others of a more general social nature are also encouraged: "associations for giving mutual aid; various agencies established by the foresight of private persons to care for the worker and likewise for his dependent wife and children in the event that an accident, sickness or death befalls him; and foundations to care for boys and girls, for adolescents, and for the aged" (RN, 68). Groups which combine forces and elaborate plans for increasing the prosperity of both families and individuals are "lawfully associated bodies of citizens," in whose affairs the state must not interfere. These groups, even as they are freely formed, so also "have the right freely to adopt the organization and the rules which they judge most appropriate to achieve their purpose" (RN, 75–76).

Within the limits of the common good, the social activity of these associations remains the result of free initiative of the citizens; it is a "vital activity . . . set in motion by an inner principle" (RN, 75), which can be "very easily destroyed . . . by intrusion from without." State activity is admitted only by reason of the necessity of the juridical order and the common good.

> It is not right, as we have said, for either the citizen or the family to be absorbed by the state; it is proper that the individual and the family should be permitted to retain their freedom of action, so far as this is possible without jeopardizing the common good and without injuring anyone. Nevertheless, those who govern must see to it that they protect the community and its constituent parts . . . if, therefore, an injury has been done to or threatens either the common good or the interests of the individual groups, which injury cannot in any other way be repaired or prevented, it is necessary for the public authority to intervene (RN, 52).

Public authority and public law may intervene in social life but the right of intervention is limited, "and these limits are determined by the same reason which demands the aid of the law, that is, the law ought not undertake more nor go farther than the remedy of evils or the removal of As in the question of property, so also in the matter of the

It is in the light of this same principle of subsidiarity that Pope John's final evaluation of the fact of socialization is made.

As the interlocking organizations of modern society develop, right order will be realized more and more through a renewed balance between a demand for autonomous and active collaboration on the part of all—individuals and groups—and timely coordination and encouragement of private enterprise by government.

So long as socialization is kept within these limits of the moral order, it will not of its nature seriously restrict individuals or overburden them. Instead, it offers hope of promoting in them the expression and development of their personal characteristics. It results, too, in an organic reconstruction of society, which our predecessor Pius XI, in *Quadragesimo Anno*, put forward and defended as the indispensable prerequisite for satisfying abundantly the demands of social justice" (MM, 66–67).

CHAPTER FOUR

THE ECONOMIC COMMUNITY

As in the question of property, so also in the matter of the relationship between workers and employers in the economic community, economic liberalism and Marx's theory stand as extreme contrasts to the social doctrine of the encyclicals.

> Workers and employers should regulate their mutual relations under the inspiration of the principle of human solidarity and Christian brotherhood. This should be their principle because both competition, understood in the sense of economic Liberalism, and class struggle, taken in Marx's sense, are contrary to the nature of man and the Christian conception of life (MM, 23).

There is, moreover, an evident parallel between the principles governing the ownership of property and those which should regulate the economic order, as can be gathered from *Quadragesimo Anno*. The purpose of both ownership and economic activity is the same: to serve the needs of all (QA, 45–47); they both have a twofold aspect, individual and social (QA, 45, 57, 69); both must be socially controlled in view of the common good (QA, 49, 88).

In the exposition of the principles governing the relationship between workers and employers, there is, in the
encyclicals, an evolving moral judgment which corresponds
to the evolving social situation. Leo XIII had to defend the
right of workers to a just wage and their right to organize
for the protection of their interests. From these minimal
demands of justice to John XXIII's espousal of the "desire
of employees to participate actively in the management of
enterprises in which they are employed" (MM, 91) there is
a giant step. The positions, however, are not discontinuous.
They both correspond to legitimate demands of human
dignity "in conformity with the progressive historical
developments in the economic, social, and political fields"
(MM, 93), and between them there is a progression of
doctrine in the writings of Pius XI and Pius XII.

At the same time, elemental wage justice which was the
stark social problem at the time of *Rerum Novarum* has not
ceased to be a real concern at the writing of *Mater et Magistra*,
despite the admitted general improvement of the condition
of labor. "Our heart is filled with deep sadness in con-
templating the immeasureably sorrowful spectacle of vast
numbers of workers in many lands and entire continents
who are paid wages which condemn them and their families
to subhuman conditions of life" (MM, 68).

This lament does not apply uniformly to all sections of
the modern world. The Pope mentions in this regard workers
"in many lands and entire continents" and he indicates
reasons for the particularly acute nature of the problem in
certain areas: the modern process of industrialization is just
beginning or still insufficiently advanced; the desire in some
countries to increase the output of the national economy
at a rate which exceeds the limits permitted by justice and

humanity; the devotion of a notable share of the national income to building up excessive national prestige and to armament expenditures.

Lest we absolve our own affluent society from all guilt, however, and write off this section of the encyclical as not applying to the United States (as happened in the case of some of the directives of *Quadragesimo Anno*), the added comment should give us pause: "It not infrequently happens that in economically advanced countries great, and sometimes very great reward is paid for the performance of some small task, or one of doubtful value. At the same time, however, the diligent and profitable toil of whole classes of decent, hard working men receives a recompense that is too small, or even totally insufficient" (MM, 70). Studies such as *Poverty in America*[1] bear out the relevance of this statement to the American economic community. For this reason Pope John felt it necesary to reaffirm the traditional teaching of Leo XIII that the remuneration of work cannot be left entirely to the laws of the market nor fixed by an arbitrary decision.

There is a reminder here of the point stressed both in *Rerum Novarum* and *Quadragesimo Anno* that any simple, "single rule" solution of this complicated problem must be rejected (QA, 67; RN, 32). Such simplistic solutions were offered by socialism's doctrine of the injustice of the wage contract itself—everything being due to the workers alone—and by liberalism's claim that wages are to be regulated only by the law of supply and demand, the free consent of the contracting parties, according to the exigencies of this law, being the determinant of what is a just wage. Socialism's theory (with only a change in the identity of the employer) has defaulted in the face of economic actuality and possibility; but liberalism's position still has its defenders.

The long since discredited "iron law of wages," so named by the Socialists but enunciated by Ricardo, was the core of the Liberalist system which prevailed at the time of *Rerum Novarum:* "The natural price of labor is that price which is necessary to enable the laborers, one with another, to subsist and to perpetuate their race, without either increase or diminution."[2]

Above or below this "natural" price of labor, the "market" price, which resulted from free agreement according to the supply and demand of the labor market, might vary slightly; but the variation would be small and temporary. Automatically and necessarily it came back to this natural price of bare subsistence.

Against this patent inhumanity, which reduces human labor to the level of a material commodity, Leo XIII asserted the doctrine of a minimum just wage. Contracts between worker and employer should be free. But, because labor is both personal and necessary,

> There is always underlying such agreements an element of natural justice, and one greater and more ancient than the free consent of contracting parties, namely, that the wage shall not be less than enough to support a worker who is thrifty and upright. If, compelled by necessity or moved by fear of a worse evil a worker accepts a harder condition, which although against his will he must accept because the employer or contractor imposes it, he certainly submits to force, against which justice cries out in protest (RN, 63).

Rerum Novarum further gives solid exegetical grounds for extending this clear doctrine of a minimum living wage to a minimum family wage, which will enable a worker to provide comfortably not only for himself but for his wife and children. Such an extension is also implicit in the argument proposed by the encyclical and since evolved in natural law philosophy of the intrinsic value of a normal adult's labor power. Nevertheless this remained a point of at least academic dispute until the clarification of the doctrine by Pius XI.[3]

Quadragesimo Anno left no doubt in the matter: "In the first place, the worker must be paid a wage sufficient to support himself and his family" (QA, 71; *Divini Redemptoris*, 31). This is the first conclusion Pius XI draws from the considerations he adds to those of *Rerum Novarum* for the determination of a just wage. Leo XIII had pointed out the personal and necessary character of labor; Pius XI adds the observation that the just evaluation of work necessarily involves its social as well as its individual aspect (QA, 69). Labor is meant for the support of the worker and his family; but it also has an essentially social function, even as ownership. It is a cooperating unit, together with ownership and management, in the service of the common good; it cannot produce its fruit except in social cooperation; one man's job and wages necessarily affect the economic life of others in modern society.

From this social aspect of work *Quadragesimo Anno* sets down two more conclusions: the condition of the business must be taken into account, and wages must be adjusted to the public economic good.

Consideration of the nature of the business is two-pronged. Its principal requirement is that wage demands be not so excessive as to ruin the business, with consequent calamity to the workers. Second, the question of the inability of an employer to pay an equitable wage either through his own fault or because of unjust burdens is taken up, and principles are given for the solution of the problem in both contingencies (QA, 72, 73).

Adjustment of wages to the public economic good recalls the fact that employment is a function of wages. Unemployment will be caused by wages that are either too high or too low. Either a purchasing power theory of wages or a cost theory, if one be followed to the exclusion of the other, leads to the same result. Consequently wages and salaries must be so adjusted "as to offer to the greatest possible number the opportunity of getting work and obtaining suitable means of livelihood." Social justice requires a "maximum employment wage" (QA, 74).

It should be noted here that the encyclicals never attempt a concrete monetary expression of the just wage. This would be beyond the scope of the exposition of principles which is the object of the encyclicals; it is rather the work of economists, businessmen, and union officials who must apply these principles at the bargaining table. *Mater et Magistra* appositely remarks:

> It is clear that these standards of judgment are valid always and everywhere. However, the degree to which they are applicable to concrete cases cannot be determined without reference to the available wealth. This wealth, to be sure, can—and in fact does—vary in quantity and quality from country to country and even, under changing circumstances, within the same country (MM, 72).

This concrete determination of what wages should be is a part of the problem of the distribution of growing wealth. In this regard the emphatic conclusion reached by the encyclicals is that economic activity can be properly rewarded, even as it can be properly directed, only when the economic system is considered as a humanly directed whole. It cannot be left to mechanically operating laws of the market. A right proportion between wages and salaries, between profits and wages, between prices and wages, between the prices obtained by various sectors of the economy— agriculture, industry, services—must be maintained. Such a proportion calls for "agreement of plans and wills" in which the guiding beacon must be the common good (QA, 75; MM, 79).

The wage contract, under these conditions, can be legitimate and just, but it is clear from *Quadragesimo Anno* that it is not an ideal arrangement. It has obvious disadvantages that accentuate the undesirable qualities of our industrial society. It tends to increase friction and antagonism between workers and employers because of the subordination of one to the other. It leads to a loss of incentive and efficiency because of the separation of labor and the ownership of the means of production. For the same reason it promotes a "wage mentality"—an unwillingness to accept responsibility—and conditions workers to the apathetic acceptance of subsistence on a dole in times of economic recession. For this reason *Quadragesimo Anno* suggests that, when possible, the wage contract should be modified:

> We consider it more advisable, however, in the present condition of human society that, so far as is possible, the work contract be somewhat modified by a partnership contract, as is already being done in various ways and with no small advantage to workers and owners. Workers and other employees thus become sharers in ownership or management or participate in some fashion in the profits received (QA, 65).

This change in the wage contract is not put down as a requirement of justice; it is suggested as "advisable" in the present condition of human society. What is desired is any

reform which will bring about a closer collaboration between capital and labor. Profit sharing, employee stock
ownership, and representation of workers on boards of
directors are the suggested means.

In the teaching of *Mater et Magistra* we find this suggestion apparently raised to the level of a moral imperative.

> It follows that if the organization and operation of an
> economic system are such as to compromise the human
> dignity of those who engage in it, or to blunt their sense of
> responsibility, or to impede the exercise of personal
> initiative, such an economic system is unjust. And this is so
> even if, by hypothesis, the wealth produced through such a
> system reaches a high level and this wealth is distributed
> according to standards of justice and equity (MM, 83).

To put this teaching in proper perspective, it must be seen
in the light of the intervening development of doctrine under
Pius XII. The subject of worker-owner relations and modification of the wage contract was clarified by him on the
occasion of the codetermination disputes which occurred in
Europe after World War II.[4] His pronouncements on the
subject were contained in addresses of May 7, 1949, to the
International Union of Catholic Employers,[5] and of June
3, 1950, to the Catholic International Congresses for Social
Studies and Social Action.[6]

Codetermination (comanagement) signifies that form of
industrial organization which gives to the workers a share
in the decisions of the businessmen for whom they work.
Types of codetermination vary with the greater or lesser
extent of worker authority admitted. It may be restricted to
social or personnel decisions, involving, for instance,
conditions and hours of work, job rates and classifications,
pensions, seniority, holidays, plant discipline; or it may

extend to economic decisions, which immediately affect the owner's right to the disposal of his property, such as financing policies, production policies, plant disposal, hiring, prices, and profits.

In the United States, labor has not been interested in this latter type of economic codetermination as such, especially as the object of legislation, relying (more healthily) on a gradual extension of collective bargaining. But European labor has accepted the idea, and laws setting up Works Councils in various industries to give representation to the workers on boards of directors, such as the plant constitution law of November, 1952, in Germany, have received support from strange bedfellows. Both Catholics and Socialists have endorsed the system, though for different reasons: Catholic support being inspired by the ideal of the human dignity of the worker and of solidarity, Socialists looking on the Works Councils as instruments of political policy and a revolutionary step towards the elimination of ownership.

An overenthusiastic interpretation of the words of *Quadragesimo Anno* regarding the modification of the wage contract may have misled some German Catholics in this matter. At any rate, an exaggeration of the right of codetermination was the result. Thus the Catholic Social Conference held in Bochum, Westphalia, in September, 1949, declared: "Catholic workers and employers are agreed that the right of codetermination for all workers in social, personal, and economic questions is a natural right in the order intended by God, to which right corresponds the obligation of co-responsibility for all. We demand that this right be established by law...."[7]

This statement did not agree with the principle, enunciated by Pius XII a few months earlier, that "the owner of the means of production . . . individual owner, workers' association or cooperation, must always, within the limits of public economic law, retain control of his economic decisions."[8] The resulting confusion called for a further clarification of the problem; this came in the Pope's declaration of June 3, 1950:

> For decades now . . . a new social policy has been developing —often under the decisive influence of the Catholic Social Movement. This social policy has been characterized by a progressive evolution of labor law and, corelatively, by the subjugation of the private owner (disposing of the means of production) to juridical obligations in favor of the worker. The attempt to push social policy further in this same direction encounters a limit at the point where there arises the danger that the working class will follow, in its turn, the errors of capital. These consist in withdrawing the disposition of the means of production—principally in the very great enterprises—from the personal responsibility of the private owner (be it an individual or a company) in order to transfer it to the responsibility of anonymous collective forms. . . .
>
> A similar danger arises as well when one demands that salaried workers belonging to an enterprise should have the right of economic comanagement, especially when the exercise of this right depends in fact, directly or indirectly, on organizations managed outside the enterprise. For neither the nature of the contract of work nor the nature of the enterprise necessarily implies a right of this kind. It is indisputable that the salaried worker and the employer are equally subjects, not objects, of the economy of a people. There is no question of denying this equality. It is a principle that social policy has already validated and that a policy organized according to professions would make still more efficacious. But there is nothing in the relations of private law, in so far as they are ruled by the simple wage contract, which would be in contradiction with that fundamental parity.[9]

It is important to note what is said and what is not said in this statement.

The Pope does not deny the desirability of workers participating in the affairs of the individual enterprise. In fact he has elsewhere approved of this: "The church looks favorably upon and encourages everything that tends to introduce elements of a contract of partnership in the labor contract."[10]

He says nothing of "social codetermination," assuming this as a requisite of human dignity. His concern is unlimited economic codetermination; and with regard to this he denies any right, on the level of the individual enterprise, founded on the nature of the work contract, or on the nature of the enterprise, or on the human equality of workers and employers. Human dignity, which makes all men equally the subjects, not the objects, of the "economy of a people," gives labor and capital a "fundamental parity" on the level of the national economy, by reason of which both should have an equal voice in the direction of the whole economic system. But this equality on the level of professional organization (recalling the vocational groups or "orders" of *Quadragesimo Anno*) does not demand equality at the plant level.

The rejection of these grounds, however, as founding a right of economic codetermination does not involve a rejection of codetermination itself. Grave misgivings are expressed as to any codetermination which would be exercised by anonymous organizations managed outside the enterprise (by unions for example) rather than by the workers themselves. But these misgivings concern not codetermination itself but the form it takes. It would defeat the very purpose of codetermination, which is to foster personal responsibility. Anonymity of management (and, therefore, of comanagement) had been condemned long before by *Quadragesimo Anno* as an occasion of irresponsibility, injustice, and fraud.

Pope Pius merely denies any right to such codetermination as necessarily implied in any of the three abovementioned considerations by themselves. He does not say that there can be no grounds at all for economic codetermination. The possibility of the introduction of such organization by law, in the event that the common good should require it, or that it should result from a free agreement between employer and employees, is still open.

A final noteworthy point in Pius XII's treatment of this matter is the distinction he makes between smaller enterprises, where the concept of owner still connotes control, and larger concerns, in which separation of ownership and control prevails. Codetermination is suggested for the latter:

> Small and average sized undertaking in agriculture, in the arts and crafts, in commerce and industry, should be safeguarded and fostered by allowing them to share in the advantages of larger firms through entry into cooperative unions; in the large concerns, meanwhile, there should be the possibility of modifying the work contract by one of partnership.[11]

The inclusion of this citation at the beginning of the section of *Mater et Magistra* which treats of the participation of labor in the decisions of the enterprise in which they are employed, bears out the contention that John XXIII's teaching must be interpreted in the light of what Pius XII has said.

This continuity and evolution are evident with regard to the fundamental requirements of justice in wages. The same individual, familial, and social norms that are set down in previous encyclicals are reaffirmed in *Mater et Magistra*. But *Mater et Magistra* advances the doctrine in two ways. First, it spells out in some detail the "consideration of the common good" which *Quadragesimo Anno* had declared essential to the determination of wage justices (MM, 79). Second, and perhaps more significantly, faithful to its repeated insistence on the intensifying unity of mankind in the modern world, the encyclical extends this normative common good beyond the nation to include that of the international order. The avoidance of unfair competition between the economies of different countries, the encouragement of collaboration among national economies, effective cooperation in the economic development of underdeveloped nations are now, in view of the contemporary international situation, factors in the determination of both wages and profit (MM, 78, 80).

With regard to the modification of the work contract, the element of evolution in the doctrine is, as has been indicated, startlingly clear in *Mater et Magistra*. This is consequently one of the sections of the encyclical which the ultra-conservatives found particularly unpalatable.

Pope John leaves no doubt that he defends "the desire of employees to participate actively in the management of enterprises in which they are employed" (MM, 91). In a number of varied phrases he endorses this active participation: the opportunity for those engaged in production to exercise responsibility is described as "an innate demand of human nature" (MM, 82); workers should be allowed to acquire shares in the firms in which they are employed, this being one of the "most desirable" ways of satisfying "a demand of justice" (MM, 75); workers "must not be kept entirely passive with regard to the making of decisions that regulate their activity," rather they "should have a timely say in and be able to make a welcome contribution to the efficient development of the enterprise" (MM, 92). The desire of workers to exercise responsibility in productive units is declared to correspond "to lawful demands inherent in human nature" (MM, 93).

The continuity of this development should not be overlooked. Pope John asserts that in it he is following the line of thought of his predecessors. Nothing is said in *Mater et Magistra* which contradicts the teaching of Pius XII in the matter of codetermination. Nowhere does John XXIII claim economic codetermination as a natural right or as one necessarily springing from the work contract. At most it is spoken of as "a desire" of employees which should be allowed.

The difference between the positions of Pius XII and John XXIII is a difference between what is said and what is not said. Whereas Pius assumed the right of social codetermination, John explicitly asserts it. And whereas Pius left the actuation of economic codetermination through agreement an open question, John vigorously urges it for some situations.

Clearly *Mater et Magistra* does not prescribe economic codetermination as a universal formula. The possibility is denied of describing in detail the kind of economic organization most conformed to the dignity of man and most suited to developing his sense of responsibility. The desire of workers to participate in the management of enterprises is defended, but: "it is not feasible to define a priori the manner and extent of participation of this sort. Such matters must be decided with an eye to specific conditions prevailing in each enterprise. These conditions may vary from enterprise to enterprise, and, indeed, within the same enterprise frequently undergo sudden and profound changes" (MM, 91; 84).

Nor is the participation of which *Mater et Magistra* speaks necessarily understood as economic codetermination. The "injustice" involved in a system which compromises the dignity of the worker, blunts his sense of responsibility, and impedes personal initiative is not uniquely remedied by coownership of the means of production with a consequent unlimited power of economic decision. Participation of workers in decisions "that regulate their activity" is included in social or personnel codetermination, and it in such a codetermination that *Mater et Magistra* indicates as universally required by justice. For in the same section in which this participation is urged, the encyclical remarks that "the authority and necessary efficiency associated with unity of direction" must be safeguarded (MM, 92).

Economic codetermination as distinguished from the merely social is recommended by *Mater et Magistra* for certain cases. The encyclical first of all distinguishes between smaller and larger economic units. Economic codetermination looks especially to the latter. The former, small and average-sized business enterprises, artisan enterprises and cooperatives, which involve an active owner, should be preserved. They must adapt themselves to technological changes as well as to the changing preferences of consumers. They must organize professionally; but they must also be helped by public tax and credit policies as upholding "true human values" and contributing to the advance of civilization (MM, 85–90).

With regard to larger enterprises the situation is different. Here, "the workers should be allowed to acquire shares in the firms in which they are employed." And a further particular situation is singled out, namely, that wherein a company is expanding through a process of internal financing and in which the workers are paid no more than the minimum salary (MM, 75).

The logic behind this position is the logic of the changed meaning of ownership in individual capitalism and corporate capitalism. The entrepreneur in the corner grocery store and the stockholder in United States Steel are both called owners. But the title is used in two greatly different meanings. The individual owner-manager is the active cause of the increase of capital value as well as of the profits of his enterprise. He works, assumes responsibility, gives direction, and exercises control over his enterprise which entitles him to appropriate the increase after paying expenses. The stockholder, on the other hand, is one of a million "holders," as their name implies. And his holding usually means no more to him than a claim on profits. Increase in the value of the corporation and expansion of production do not result from his efforts but from the efforts and skill of labor and management. Yet the inactive member of a joint stock company is assumed to have the same title to this increase as the individual owner who also combines in himself the contributions of labor and management.

Given the growing conviction of the dignity of labor and the disaffection for socio-economic privilege, the modern economic community becomes increasingly restive with this anomaly. *Mater et Magistra* even applies the term "injustice" precisely in this connection, quoting the words of *Quadragesimo Anno:* "It is flagrantly unjust that either [capital or labor] should deny the efficacy of the other and seize all the profits" (MM, 76). The encyclical goes on to say:

Experience suggests that this demand of justice can be met in many ways. One of these, and among the most desirable, is to see to it that the workers, in the manner that seems most suitable, are able to participate in the ownership of the enterprise itself. For today more than in the times of our predecessor every effort . . . must be made that at least in the future a just share only of the fruits of production be permitted to accumulate in the hands of the wealthy, and that a sufficiently ample share be supplied to the working men (MM, 77).

Expressions of shock at the novelty of this proposal are unwarranted. It is not new, nor is it a sudden surrender to socialism. Akin to this program, for instance, is the suggestion once made by Monsignor John Ryan, in explaining the Christian tradition of ownership, that owners of stock be given a fixed return on their shares.[12] In this way they would be treated much like bond-holders, although receiving a slightly higher rate of return because of the greater risk involved. But then the surplus profits should be transferred from the capitalist owner to the wage earners and management. Or, to take an instance from even more authoritative sources, the bishops of the United States as far back as 1919 criticized the American Federation of Labor's program of social reform because it did not imply that labor should aspire to the ownership of the means of production.[13]

As has been said, there is, nevertheless, a giant step from the position of Leo XIII to that of John XXIII. It covers the distance between a courageous defense of fundamental human rights, in an economic world that was indifferent or hostile, and the aggressive assertion of full human dignity, in a world that now generally accepts that notion. The tone and attitude of each are conformed to the needs and the possible hopes of their differing situations. Pope John's whole approach is epitomized by his words in *Pacem in Terris:* "If a man becomes conscious of his rights, he must become equally aware of his duties. Thus, he who possesses certain rights has likewise the duty to claim those rights as a mark of his dignity, while all others have the obligation to acknowledge those rights and respect them" (PT, 44).

John's aggressiveness, however, is not an invitation to conflict. The irenic temper of his writings and words is an acknowledged trait. He is not seeking to eliminate ownership nor to expropriate the expropriators. An industrial vendetta scarcely describes the "joint effort—principally in the field of collective bargaining" for which he praises modern unions (MM, 97). Even as *Quadragesimo Anno* intended modification of the wage contract, so *Mater et Magistra* insists on the participation of all in the management of the enterprise for the purpose of introducing more intimate cooperation between capital and labor. Industrial enterprises should "assume the characteristics of a true human community" (MM, 71).

In this regard, one is struck by the recurrence of "responsibility" as the dominating theme of this whole discussion in *Mater et Magistra*. It is a constant refrain which accompanies every mention of participation in the affairs of the enterprise. The reason for this emphasis is clear.

All through the encyclicals of Pope John, the center and focus of attention is the dignity of the human person; the index of this dignity is responsibility. For a human person can best be defined as the responsible agent for his own perfection. Therefore anything that blunts a man's sense of responsibility, or impedes the opportunity of exercising responsibility, or reduces man to the level of a silent performer, or prevents the exercise of initiative (to use some of the phrases of *Mater et Magistra*) compromises the dignity of the human person.

Consequently, a condition of economic organization which makes the exercise of responsibility the prerogative of capital alone and reduces labor to an entirely passive role with regard to decision making is something less than human Human dignity demands that responsibility, as well as material gain, be shared by both capital and labor. Thus the whole problem of the economic community is raised above the level of the merely material division of the product and situated on the specifically human level of a common social function.

Duties as well as rights are at issue here. John XXIII admonishes both capital and labor: they are not competitors for the biggest piece of the economic pie; they are human cooperators in a common undertaking. And all the members of the enterprise must look on their work "not merely as a source of income, but also as the fulfillment of a duty and the performance of a service to others" (MM, 92).

This is reminiscent of the teaching of *Quadragesimo Anno* with regard to the establishment of vocational groups as a necessary element of social reconstruction, and it points to the consideration of the economic community in a wider perspective than that of the wage contract. According to Pius XI, the inspiring motive for the formation of vocational bodies or "orders" was the fact of the bond of unity between capital and labor in the performance of a common function, which had been destroyed by historical capitalism's idolatry of competition. The grave evil that divides human society into a battlefield of conflicting and hostile classes must be cured by the constitution of "well ordered members of the

social body . . . in which men have their place not according
to the position each has in the labor market but according
to the respective social function which each performs"
(QA, 83).

Pius XI describes these well-ordered members of the
social body in some detail: they correspond, under forms
adapted to the present day, to the ancient guilds (*Divini
Redemptoris*, 54; their unifying force is already "present"
in the common good of the same industry or profession of
the members, and the common good of the whole country to
which their occupation contributes (QA, 84); they extend
beyond the limits of a particular plant or company, embracing all the members of an identical profession; in them,
because they are thus considered on the level of the whole
economy, capital and labor enjoy equality (a "fundamental
parity," to repeat the words of Pius XII); they are self-
governing and possess autonomy within the structure of the
state (QA, 84); their actuation results in an organic structuring of society, uniting men according to the functions they
perform rather than dividing them according to class
(QA, 83, 90); and finally they make possible the
application of the principle of subsidiarity (QA, 78, 82).

It has been pointed out that this reorganization of the
social order along the lines of vocational groups, which
holds such a prominent place in *Quadragesimo Anno*, is given
very brief mention in *Mater et Magistra*, and it has further
been suggested that the plan is played down in this later
encyclical. Such a judgment does an injustice to Pope John.

The term, "vocational group,"[14] is not used in *Mater et
Magistra*, but the ideas and principles of the plan are in
evidence. If we might attempt a summary of these principles:

    1. Economic activity should not be left to absolutely

free competition. It must be controlled in view of the common good.

2. Nevertheless, this does not mean that the state should regulate all. The economy is the creation of individuals and groups within the state resulting from the personal initiative of the citizens. The role of the state is subsidiary.

3. Intermediate groups, therefore, enjoying effective autonomy, and springing from the natural sociability of men, should affect the direction of the economy in accord with the demands of the common good.

4. In these groups, beyond the confines of individual productive units, both Capital and Labor should be represented.

Whatever lack of evidence there is in *Mater et Magistra*, it does not stifle the resonance of these principles of social order. The ideal of an organic, as opposed to an atomistic, structure of society, which was the goal of Pius XI's "vocational groups," is accepted and endorsed by Pope John (MM, 67). But there is no suggestion in *Mater et Magistra* of any rigid form in which that ideal is to be embodied. Actually, of course, neither did Pope Pius ever intend to freeze social organization in an inflexible framework (QA, 86–87; DR, 54). This, however, was the conclusion reached by some interpretations of the term "vocational group." Such interpretations were a cogent reason for John's avoidance of the term.

"The basic elements of the fundamental social reform advocated in earlier papal writings," Father John Cronin remarks in *The Social Teaching of Pope John XXIII* (Milwaukee, Bruce, 1963), p. 23, "as summarized in this encyclical, have permanent validity. Too often, however, impractical commentators used them to build blueprints of a rigidly controlled economy. . . . Pope John preferred to emphasize the spirit behind this reform, and he did this by insisting upon social responsibility and the principle of subsidiarity. If these ideals control social-reform movements, they will move in the direction advocated by Pope Pius XI. His goals will be achieved, but in various ways according to the history, temperament and culture of different national economies. This flexibility was advocated in *Quadragesimo Anno.* Pope John was simply an accurate interpreter of his predecessor."

CHAPTER FIVE

THE POLITICAL COMMUNITY

The following words of Vatican Council II afford a summary
of the moral judgment of the encyclicals of John XXIII on
the contemporary political situation:

> It is in full accord with human nature that juridical-political
> structures should . . . afford all their citizens the chance to
> participate freely and actively in establishing the con-
> stitutional basis of a political community, governing the state,
> determining the scope and purpose of various institutions,
> and choosing leaders. Hence, let all citizens be mindful of
> their simultaneous right and duty to vote freely in the interest
> of advancing the common good.[1]

Even as in the economic community, which has previously
been discussed, so in the political community the aspiration
of all citizens to a share in responsibility is natural, legitimate, and, in the light of changing attitudes, strongly encouraged.

This encouragement marks the development of the
political philosophy of *Pacem in Terris* over that of *Rerum
Novarum*. The naturalness and legitimacy of popular participation in government and in the shaping of public policy,

which are the functions of politics, has never been questioned in Catholic political tradition.

It is often forgotten that this doctrine was a common-place of medieval philosophy. "The fact that in medieval theory," says Carlyle,[2] "the authority of the King is founded upon the election or at least the recognition of the community, does not in truth demand any serious demonstration." The best form of government, according to St. Thomas,[3] was "mixed," in which all would have some part in governing and in which those holding power could be elected from and by the people. Filmer,[4] writing in defense of the Divine Right of Kings against Bellarmine and Suarez, asserted frankly that the tenet that mankind is at liberty to choose what form of government it pleases and that political power is first bestowed according to the discretion of the multitude "was first hatched in the schools, and has been fostered by all succeeding papists for good divinity."

Nor did Leo XIII depart from this tradition. Rather he affirms it in several of his encyclicals:

> No one of the several forms of government is in itself con-demned, in as much as none of them contains anything contrary to Catholic doctrine, and all of them are capable, if wisely and justly managed, of insuring the welfare of the state. Neither is it blameworthy in itself, in any manner, for the people to have a share, greater or less, in the government; for at certain times, and under certain laws, such participa-tion may not only be of benefit to the citizens, but may even be of obligation.[5]

This statement compares with a similar permissive statement of *Pacem in Terris:* "It is thus clear that the doctrine which we have set forth is fully consonant with any truly democra-tive regime" (PT, 52).

Yet throughout the writing of Leo one senses a caution with regard to democracy which contrasts with the positive encouragement of Pope John. Whereas Leo admitted the participation of the people in government as not "blameworthy in itself," John asserts that "it is in keeping with their dignity as persons that human beings should take an active part in government" (PT, 73). Government and civil authority had a more remote and paternalistic coloring in the teaching of Leo. Those who rule should rule "not as masters but rather as fathers," and the people should give dutiful homage to "the majesty of the law" and show reverence and fealty to their rulers together with "a love not unlike that which children show their parents" (*Immortale Dei*, p. 427). In contrast is Pope John's more juridically conceived form of government in which the procedures by which the governing powers are to be designated and limited are constitutionally determined (PT, 68, 76).

Again, though involvement in public life is "in general fitting and salutary," according to Leo, yet "it may in some places be true that, for most urgent and just reasons, it is by no means expedient for Catholics to engage in public affairs or to take an active part in politics" (*Immortale Dei*, p. 446). (This warning was extended to participation in associations of workers which were not Christian [RN, 74]). On the other hand, Pope John, steering clear of any Catholic ghettoism, reminds Catholics "of their duty to take an active part in public life and to contribute toward the attainment of the common good of the entire human family as well as to that of their own political community" (PT, 46; MM, 254 ff.). Further, he urges Catholics to cooperate with others who do not share their view of life (always avoiding compromises in matters of religion or morality) in a spirit of understanding and disinterestedness in achieving objectives that are of their nature good or at least reducible to good (MM, 239; PT, 158).

The difference in attitude between Pope Leo and Pope John again springs from the different circumstances of the times in which they wrote. In *Pacem in Terris*, Pope John writes:

> The modern world, as compared with the recent past, has taken on an entirely new appearance in the field of social and political life . . . thus, in our day, in very many human beings the inferiority complex which endured for hundreds and thousands of years is disappearing, while in others there is an attenuation and gradual fading of the corresponding superiority complex which had its roots in socio-economic privileges, sex, or political standing . . . on the contrary, the conviction that all men are equal by reason of their natural dignity has been generally accepted (PT, 42–44).

Remembering the disasters of two world wars and the autocratic and totalitarian systems that precipitated them, people are persuaded with good reason that effective guarantees of peace must be found in the possibility of popular control of public authorities. They will not accept political power which cannot be opposed, nor be treated as irrational pieces on a chessboard. "The peoples have, as it were, awakened from a long torpor. They have assumed, in relation to the state and those who govern, a new attitude—one that questions, criticizes, distrusts."[6]

This desire to participate in political life is now an expression of the legitimate desire to exercise responsibility as human persons in a common human endeavor. It is not an attempt to impose a false ideology on social life. And therein is the differentiating condition of the times of Pope Leo and Pope John. *Pacem in Terris* indicates this differentiation:

It must be borne in mind, furthermore, that neither can false philosophical teachings regarding the nature, origin, and destiny of the universe and of man be identified with historical movements that have economic, social, cultural, or political ends, not even when these movements have originated from those teachings and have drawn and still draw inspiration therefrom.

This is so because the teachings, once they are drawn up and defined, remain always the same, while the movements, working in constantly evolving historical situations, cannot but be influenced by these latter and cannot avoid, therefore, being subject to changes, even of a profound nature. Besides, who can deny that those movements, in so far as they conform to the dictates of right reason and are interpreters of the lawful aspirations of the human person, contain elements that are positive and deserving of approval? (PT, 159).

It is possible in some instances, according to this distinction between historical movements and false philosophical teachings, to separate what is "positive and true" in the movements from the philosophy in which they may have originated and from which they may still draw inspiration. This recalls the observation that Pius XI made with regard to the historical evolution of socialism since the time of Leo XIII and its split into extreme and more moderate sections (both of which, however, retain their fundamentally anti-Christian position). The more moderate section, he declares, "terrified by its own principles and by the conclusions drawn therefrom by Communism, inclines toward and in a certain measure approaches the truths which Christian tradition has always held sacred; for it cannot be denied that its demands at times come very near those that Christian reformers of society justly insist upon" (QA, 113).

The distinction of *Pacem in Terris* may be a further

development of this observation of Pope Pius, and may mark, as has been frequently suggested, a new approach to practical dialogue with Communists, as distinguished from communism. But certainly, in view of Pope John's endorsement of popular participation in government, the distinction has a bearing on the noted advance of his political thinking over that of Leo XIII. In this regard, John Courtney Murray remarks:

> I should think that the distinction may be given full application in regard to the eighteenth- and nineteenth-century movements toward political freedom. So applied, the distinction dissolves the whole problematic of Leo XIII, whose great conflict was with continental, sectarian Liberalism. In his time he was not able to draw a distinction between the animating principle of this movement, which was that of the "outlaw conscience" that recognized no authority higher than itself and no law that was not of its own making and the free political institutions of which this movement was the protagonist. At this distance from the nineteenth-century state of the question, which is now outworn, John XXIII is able boldly to make this important distinction.[7]

Without a doubt, the preoccupation of Pope Leo was the naturalism and rationalism which had inspired the political liberalism of the preceding century. He closes his encyclical on the Christian constitution of states with the warning that there can be no truckling "with opinions verging on naturalism or rationalism, the essence of which is utterly to sterilize Christianity, and to instill in society the supremacy of man to the exclusion of God" (I D, p. 448). His concern was with the disastrous effects of this philosophy on the life of the political community.

The problem of the political community is the problem, previously mentioned in the discussion of "socialization," of the reconciliation of liberty and authority in the pursuit of the common good. It is in the juridical order of the political community, or civil society, that the other associations which we spoke of as growing out of the natural sociability of man—the economic, cultural, recreational, social, and professional associations—find their larger unity in cooperation for the common good of them all, the common good of the *polis*. Such unity, to be effective, necessarily requires a supreme political authority; but to be truly political it supposes freedom. Political power is a power over free men. "Human society is realized in freedom, that is to say, by ways and means in keeping with the dignity of its citizens, who accept the responsibility of their actions precisely because they are by nature rational beings" (PT, 35).

The intellectual poverty of continental liberalism which Leo opposed and its practical impotence to solve this problem has already been indicated. Its antithetical conception of liberty and authority prohibited such a solution and logically offered an ultimate choice between license and regimentation. The dilemma is still a concern. Orton remarks in *The Liberal Tradition:* "There is no more urgent task for modern Liberalism than to clarify the concepts of authority on the one hand and democracy on the other; for our wretched state is due in no small measure to the flagrant misunderstanding and practical abuse of both."[8]

Dazzled by the wonder of the free will of man, liberalism denied the dependence of human freedom. Liberalism found, as we have said, the dignity of man in his independence of any authority outside himself—a concept popularized by half-true slogans which somehow were taken as axiomatic refutations of authority: dogmas fetter the human spirit;

man is the captain of his soul and the master of his fate; that
government is best which governs least; free enterprise is the
soul of progress.

The development of liberalism in its process of liber-
ating the human spirit from the thraldom of authority
was gradual. By way of preparation came the liberation
from the religious authority of Rome and the Pope. The
Encyclopedia of the Social Sciences cites the Reformation of the
sixteenth century as "the most important factor in revital-
izing the stoic doctrine of the primacy of the individual
and in giving new emphasis to individual rights as a
separate and distinct subject of liberty."[9] At this point, the
freedom gained was that of the right of private judgment
in matters of religion, misnamed freedom of conscience.
It still was a dependent freedom and a dependent conscience, acknowledging the authority of God, but denying
any human authoritative interpreter of faith and morals
intervening between the individual conscience and God.

The event proved that the Reformation was anything but
"liberal." It did, however, destroy, for a great portion of the
world, the authority of the Church. But with the destruction
of that authority it gave rise to a new (and real) menace to
human freedom: the power of the state.[10] Heretofore
restrictions and curbs had held state absolutism in check.
The accepted moral authority of the Church had governed
ruler and ruled alike. Now it governed neither. Nationalism
grew; the "Divine Right of Kings" appeared.[11] Political
absolutism reappeared. The medieval ideas restricting regal
absolutism—the ideas of the participation of all in government,[12] of the tempering of regal power to prevent tyrannical
abuse,[13] of tyranny as a violation of a pact between ruler
and subjects[14]—were abandoned.

Luther's pessimistic doctrine of the corruption of human nature gave theoretical support to the new order. The state came from God; not, however, produced by man's reason and will, subject to the natural law, but as instituted by divine providence on account of sin. Temporal princes were the instruments of God's anger to punish and keep peace.[15] Nor could there be any recourse to natural law against the injustice of the law of the state.[16]

Opposed to this state absolutism a new liberation became the object of eighteenth-century liberalism: political liberation. By way of preparation came the rationalism and naturalism of the Enlightenment, which mediated the transformation of the "free conscience" into the "outlaw conscience." Reason replaced revelation; man replaced God. Everything was to be judged at the bar of human reason, nothing was to be accepted that reason could not prove. Reason was all-powerful to understand the laws of nature and to guide mankind to unlimited progress, if only it were freed of the trammels of religion and the established political order.

The philosophers of the Enlightenment were anti-Christian and anti-religious. They rejected divine law, the authority of God, and some—not all—rejected His existence. With this rejection they also eschewed the notion of political authority as derived from God. There was no political power except such as originated in the wills of the governed.

Unfortunately for the course of history, the political situation of the time involved what was in reality a perversion of the traditional Christian doctrine of the divine origin of authority. This travesty led to the denial of the derivation of authority from God. Not only was there no divine right

of kings, but henceforth there was to be no divine right.
Religion was relegated to the privacy of individual life. Man
and man's reason were sufficient for social life. The will
of the people would establish all laws and appoint their
administrators, thus assuring freedom and equality to all the
members of the political community.

Enlightened self-interest would take the place of well-
ordered self-love, and the deistic power which "has bid
self-love and social be the same," rather than the moral
obligation of social cooperation, would automatically (and
optimistically) direct the course of political society. The
"general will," which finds its voice in the mechanics of a
majority vote, could have no interest contrary to the interest
of any individual, since it is composed of all.

The sophism of this explanation of popular power and
its inherent totalitarian trend are evident.[17] But—and
this is the position of Pope John—it is not necessarily
implied in any and every acceptance of democracy. Philosophical rationalism is no more essential to a program of
political democracy than Marxist atheism is to a program
for a just distribution of the goods of the world.

Mater et Magistra and *Pacem in Terris*, therefore, addressed
themselves principally to the political philosophy which
must be expressed in a healthy democratic regime. They are
interested not so much in the external form of political
society, which may vary with the historical background and
circumstances of given political communities and with their
level of development (PT, 67, 68, 73), but with the principle,
enunciated by Pius XII,[18] that the human person is not an
object or a merely passive element in the social order but
rather its subject, its foundation, and its end. Here again
we are presented with the touchstone of all right order, the

dignity of the human person. Man is not the object of alien manipulation and use; he is, in a true sense, sacred.

Man's sacredness, however, is founded neither in a complete autonomy nor in a splendid isolation which must compromise with the hard fact that solitary existence is impossible. Either option would deny his very being as an essentially social creature of God.

Man's being is dependent and so also is the freedom which distinguishes him. Man is not being; rather he *has* being which has been communicated to him by God. His perfection consists in the reception of perfection. His freedom is not a negative immunity from constraint or limitation, it is the positive power of self-realization within the order of his divinely given nature—the ultimate responsibility for accepting or refusing the gift of being.

Man's dignity consists in the fact that he is made in the image of God. To man has been given a share in the creation of the world. His is the responsibility of bringing it to its perfection, of cultivating it, of investigating its forces and harnessing them for his own benefit (PT, 2, 3). Above all, in imitation of the Creator (how much more by reason of his supernatural participation in the trinitarian life of God!) man must share and communicate life with others, for without this communication he fails in his creative role. This is but another way of saying that, by the order of creation, man is meant to live in society which has as its purpose the responsible development of the potentialities of rational nature by means of coordinated and mutually supplementary action.

It is in the light of these reflections that *Mater et Magistra* and *Pacem in Terris* seek the solution of the apparent antinomy of liberty and authority. Quite evidently the problem involves the question of the origin and the scope of political authority. The thesis which holds for a human origin of that authority and its consequent essential indetermination, as we have mentioned, renders liberalism's attempted solution sterile. The resolution must be sought in the divine source of both the dignity of the individual person and the social order without which his life is less than human.

Pope John draws heavily on the teaching of Leo XIII, Pius XI, and Pius XII in reaffirming this completely traditional position:

> Since God made man social by nature, and since no society can hold together unless someone be over all, directing all to strive earnestly for the common good, every civilized community must have a ruling authority, and this authority, no less than society itself, has its source in nature, and has, consequently, God for its author (PT, 46).

Subordination to authority thus derived from God is not a negation of human liberty, which is a dependent liberty. It is rather a perfection of that liberty, which must also be responsible (PT, 50). In view of the necessity of society as a condition of human perfection and of the necessity of coordinated activity for the prosperity of society, subordination to authority in its essential function of assuring the common good is a moral good, not a necessary evil.

> That same absolute order of being and their ends which presents man as an autonomous person, that is, as the subject of inviolable duties and rights, and as at once the basis of society and the purpose for which it exists, also includes the state as a necessary society invested with authority without which it could not come into being or live . . . and since this absolute order—as we learn from sound reason, and especially from Christian faith—can have no origin save in a personal God who is our Creator, it follows that the dignity

of the state's authority is due to its sharing to some extent in the authority of God Himself (PT, 47).

In all this, it is clear that there is question here of political authority itself, "the power to command according to right reason" (PT, 47), which must be an attribute of any civil society; it is not a question of its concrete form or personal location. The absolute order of beings and their ends, which "can have no origin save in a personal God who is our Creator," must be distinguished from the contingent order, wherein men have the right "to choose who are to rule the state, to decide the form of government, and to determine both the way in which authority is to be exercised and its limits" (PT, 52).

It is this same "absolute order," being the order of natural ends, which also determines the scope of political authority in view of its purpose. That purpose is the care of the common good. "The whole reason for the existence of civil authority is the realization of the common good" (PT, 54).

There is hardly an issue more crucial for social weal or woe than this notion of the common good, "a sound view of the common good" which *Mater et Magistra* cites as necessary for the control of the modern phenomenon of socialization (MM, 65). The critical importance of this notion, as well as the ambiguity of the term, is illustrated by the social aberrations of individualism and collectivism.

The common good is not merely the "greatest good of the greatest number." It is not a matter of numbers, of a majority (although quantitative considerations may be a criterion of its non-realization); it is a good of the whole social body, a good of all. Nor is the common good a stock-pile of goods offered equally to all, from which all may take according to their needs; it must always respect the self-provident responsibility of the human person. Nor again does it consist in an abundance of public institutions such as hospitals, roads, research foundations, although these are instruments of the common good; such institutions may abound in a society which suppresses the dignity and legitimate freedom of its members.

Clarification of the content of the common good, and consequent determination of the scope and limits of authority is, therefore, in the light of the necessarily extended activity of government in modern society (MM, 54), an expected development of *Mater et Magistra* and *Pacem in Terris* in their treatment of the political community.

Generically, "the common good of all embraces the sum total of those conditions of social living whereby men are enabled to achieve their own integral perfection more perfectly and more easily" (PT, 58). A good in itself, a "good of all" distinct from "individual good," it is nevertheless an enabling good, a means for the responsible self-development of the human person. This recalls the admonition of *Quadragesimo Anno* that "every social activity ought of its very nature to furnish help to the members of the social body and never destroy or absorb them" (QA, 78).

More in detail, the common good, as an effect of social collaboration, is an external good, but it "touches on the whole man" (PT, 57), embracing both the material and the spiritual welfare of the citizens. It is the result of the responsible cooperation of each citizen, demanding that individual citizens and intermediate groups within the national community make their specific contributions (PT, 53). It involves respect for the cultural contributions of various ethnic groups (PT, 55). It requires that the intermediate groups, pursuing the cooperative attainment of cultural, economic, professional, and political ends "should enjoy affective autonomy" (MM, 60, 65). But it also embraces supplementary public contributions of the higher society when, and to the extent that, the intermediate groups are unequal to their social task (MM, 53–55; PT, 65).

Most fundamentally, the common good consists in the guarantee of personal rights and duties, and their regulation and coordination, so that the exercise of one man's right does not threaten others in the exercise of their own rights and duties (PT, 62). Performance of civic duty as well as the inviolability of individual rights are equally parts of the common good. They are constantly coupled in the explanations of the encyclicals. The common good is realized insofar as individuals can easily exercise their rights and fulfill their duties in every sector of social life (PT, 63, 66).

The common good is thus understood as "the order of society in which every member enjoys the possibility of realizing his true self by participating in the cooperation of all."[19] It is ultimately reduced to an effective juridical order of defined and protected mutual rights and duties, and a flourishing social order of mutual complementation by the interchange and communication of goods of every human order.

These two constituents of the common good objectively determine the extent and limits of civil authority whose special function is to assure that common good. *Pacem in Terris* (65) sums up the task of political authority in the "coordinating," "protecting," and "promoting" of the rights of the citizens. "To safeguard the inviolable rights of the human person, and to facilitate the fulfillment of his duties should be the essential office of every public authority" (PT, 66).

Within the security of this juridical order, guaranteed by public authority, the production and exchange of that abundance and variety of goods and services necessary for a full human life are (as *Mater et Magistra* remarks with specific reference to the economy) "the creation of the personal initiative of private citizens. It results from their pursuit of common interests either as individuals or in various associations" (MM, 51).

In this order of social cooperation, political authority can intervene only to make it more effective. The state with its authority may intervene, if necessary, for the coordination and regulation of private social relations, indicated above as an element of the common good. Or authority may intervene to supply the goods and services which cannot be provided by private enterprise (PT, 62, 63, 66; MM, 52–55).

Especially acute today is this problem of the supplementary intervention of public authority in the social life of the people. There always have been, and always will be, differences of opinion, sincere differences about the application of this principle of subsidarity. But the problem has a new urgency today, as *Mater et Magistra* and *Pacem in Terris* point out, for several reasons. "Recent advances in scientific knowledge and productive technology provide public authorities with far greater capacities than in the past for reducing inequalities among various sectors of production . . . and put it within their competence to control fluctuations in the economy and to bring effective remedies to bear on the problem of mass unemployment" (MM, 54). Again, the variety, complexity, and dynamic character of social life in the modern world is such that it cannot be regulated by inflexible legal provisions (PT, 71–72). The result of these factors is that those in authority responsible for the common good are more and more required to undertake a variety of activities, and to take action quickly and effectively to meet the exigencies of the changing social scene. This same "ever widening activity which the common good requires that public authorities undertake" is the explanation of the modern tendency toward a progressive transfer of property to the state or other agencies of public law (MM, 117).

The encyclicals of Pope John establish no new principle for the regulation of this growing government activity. New principles are not required; but the changing times call for new applications. It is for this reason that *Mater et Magistra* and *Pacem in Terris* go into much more detail than previous encyclicals in indicating areas in which government activity is legitimate. Such areas include the development of essential services such as the building of roads, transportation, communications, water supply, housing, public health, education, facilitation of the practice of religion, and recreational facilities (PT, 64; MM, 150). Social security, unemployment insurance, and employment agencies are also mentioned. Special directives are further given for the government's part in the solution of the rural problem: formulation of a prudent agricultural policy, a special credit policy for farmers, social insurance which covers both agricultural produce and the farm labor force and their families, protection of farm prices, technical assistance, and aid in the forming of cooperative and professional associations (MM, 131–146).

The measure of such government activity, however, is always the same: the necessity of the common good. These directives are "to be applied in the manner and to the degree that circumstances permit, suggest, or flatly demand" (MM, 126).

After quoting the principle of subsidiarity from *Quadragesimo Anno, Mater et Magistra* goes on to say: "This principle must always be retained: that state activity in the economic field, no matter what its breadth or depth may be, ought not to be exercised in such a way as to curtail an individual's freedom of action. Rather it should work to expand that freedom by the effective protection of each and every essential personal right" (MM, 55). And *Pacem in Terris*, repeating this principle (PT, 66), extends it to the steps that governments take "in every sector of social life."

Right order and the common good of the political community, therefore, come to realization through the cooperation of private individuals and their associations and public authority, "through a renewed balance between a demand for autonomous and active collaboration on the part of all—individuals and groups—and timely coordination and encouragement of private enterprise by government" (MM, 66).

CHAPTER SIX

THE INTERNATIONAL COMMUNITY

The radical sociability of man finds expression in constantly developing social forms. Society is the work of reason; sociability is rooted in rationality. As reason perceives ever widening possibilities of human perfection in growing social organizations, and sees the need of such organizations, if human existence is to be truly that, the very law of man's being calls for their formation. Reason is the architect of these evolving societal forms which the nature of man makes necessary.

There is, therefore, a temporal difference in the historical emergence of natural societies without any lessening of their natural character. Nor does the intervention of human reason in this historical evolution make these societies merely artificial. Specifications of natural law—here, the imperative inclination to social life—are neither automatic nor deterministic. "Socialization is not to be considered as a product of natural forces working in a deterministic way. It is, on the contrary, as we have observed, a creation of men who are free agents intended by nature to work in a responsible manner" (MM, 63).

Thus, the fundamental and primordial form of natural sociability is the family, "the first and essential cell of human society" (PT, 16), corresponding to the immediate and absolute need of man. Without it the propagation of the race and the satisfaction of the personal daily needs of man—material, spiritual, and psychological—would be impossible.

The family, however, by itself is not sufficient to enable man to realize the potentialities of his nature. It must be completed by an organization of families in cities and states—political organizations—with the purpose of security and supplementation, to protect the juridical order and supply the insufficiencies of family life.

In its turn, too, as science diminishes the distances between peoples and increases their interdependence, the inability of the nation-state to fulfill the promise of human fulfillment contained in social life becomes more apparent. A point is thus reached in this growth where a juridically structured international society endowed with an effective universal authority imposes itself as a rationally required means of further development (and even continued existence) of human well-being. Rationality does not stop at national boundaries.

Pacem in Terris advances the teachings of the social encyclicals with its unequivocal statement that this point has been reached in the evolution of the human community. The encyclical is not a political document; it is a moral guide. It does not give practical proposals for the structural changes necessary for a new international order; but it leaves no doubt about the need of these changes as demands of the "moral order itself."

At the present time no political community is able to pursue its own interests and develop itself in isolation, because its prosperity and development are both a reflection and a component part of the prosperity and development of all the other political communities (PT, 131).

. . . .

at this historical moment the present system of organization and the way its principle of authority operates on a world basis no longer correspond to the objective requirements of the universal common good (PT, 135).

"The new meaning which the common good is taking on in the historical evolution of the human family" (PT, 136) is put down by Pope John as the source of the new demand of the moral order for an institutionalized, effective worldwide authority.

What, precisely, is this "new meaning" of the common good? The common good, as *Mater et Magistra* and *Pacem in Terris* both describe it, "embraces the sum total of social living whereby men are enabled to achieve their own integral perfection more fully and easily." This concept itself is not new; nor are the elements of security, insured by authority, and prosperity, achieved by cooperation, which this definition implies. These are the common patrimony of all the social encyclicals, and, indeed, of the whole Christian tradition. Wherein, then, is the newness to be found?

Newness comes from the fact that the common good, of which John XXIII speaks, is the "universal" common good, and furthermore a universal common good which is modified by the expectancies and the perils of the "era of the atom and the conquest of space" (PT, 156), the era in which "the monstrous power of modern weapons" (PT, 111) is an ominous mark of the very period "in which the human family has already entered on its new advance toward limitless horizons" (PT, 156).

Rerum Novarum and *Quadragesimo Anno* were concerned
with the common good as the unifying principle of social
life; but the common good of which they spoke was principally the common good of the nation-state, which directly
afforded individuals and their associations the opportunity
of self-realization. Such an approach was justified by the
conditions of their times. We must remember that at the
time of *Rerum Novarum* even the local telephone was a rare
novelty, and, when Pius XI wrote, Lindbergh's flight across
the Atlantic was still a fresh memory. International communication was, as compared with today, in its infancy.

Mater et Magistra and *Pacem in Terris*, on the other hand,
while further developing the still valid concept of this
common good, continually emphasize, in the modern context of shrinking distances, the universal common good of
the entire human family. This universal common good
ultimately has the objective of "the recognition, respect,
safeguarding, and promotion of the rights of the human
person" (PT, 139), but proximately looks to the creation
"on a world basis" of an order in which the nation-states
themselves can carry out their tasks, fulfill their duties, and
exercise their rights with greater security (PT, 141).

This is not meant to imply that the universal common
good is the invention or the sudden discovery of Pope John.
"The world," as well as the family and the city, was recognized as a natural society as far back as Augustine. *Pacem
in Terris* itself introduces the discussion of the new exigencies
of the international order with a nod to this tradition of the
past: "The unity of the human family has always existed
because its members are human beings all equal by virtue
of their natural dignity. Hence there will always exist the
objective need to promote in sufficient measure the universal

common good, that is, the common good of the entire human family" (PT, 132).

To anyone familiar with papal and episcopal documents of the last fifty years,[1] this universal common good of the human family is a readily recognized refrain: there is a natural unity of all mankind, a universal brotherhood; there is a natural international law, one moral law governing both individuals and states; international community does not have to be created, it necessarily exists and has only to be organized. Excessive nationalism is repeatedly condemned as a fomenter of discord, forgetful of the brotherhood of man, and a cause of war.

The teaching of Pius XII on which John heavily relies is especially conspicuous in this accent on human solidarity. His first encyclical, *Summi Pontificatus*, gives the substance of the thought that would reappear in so many of his subsequent addresses, especially in his Christmas messages—the universal brotherhood of all men and nations.

Unity of origin, nature, and destiny are indicated by Pius XII as the sources of the natural solidarity of mankind (SP, 38). God is the Father of all; all are equal in the dignity of their rational nature; and all share the destiny of immortal life in the possession of God. Because of these bonds of unity men are not isolated units but part of a whole, the human family (SP, 42).

Moreover, this unity is not merely a metaphysical unity of specific likeness. There is a metaphysical unity of all men, but, since it is a unity of rational nature, it necessarily entails the further moral unity which is the unique expression of that nature. Rational nature possessed equally by all men immediately implies bonds of a moral law: a law of charity by which, equal in their goodness as images of God and destined for God, men are bound to love all others as they love self; and a law of justice by reason of which they must respect the dignity of all in the possession of inviolable rights.

From the very beginning of human existence, therefore, men are members of a moral community, ever coterminous with humanity itself. Justice and charity being social virtues, all men by reason of their very natures are members of the universal community of the human family; they are bound together in a brotherhood which transcends any limits of race or color or differences in physical or mental power or culture.

This universal community, congenital with mankind, is not from the beginning an organic or political society, which supposes a structured form and a supreme authority which can oblige and sanction. It is inorganic and moral, composed of equals with no institutionalized authority over all. Nor is it, despite its universality, international society in a technical sense, which supposes the formation of separate states and civil societies. But it is the foundation of both, as reason progressively develops those forms of social intercourse which the historical evolution of the human family requires.

The rational conservation of order and the implementation of the mutual aid to which the law of their nature binds them imposes on men the moral necessity of political organization. Through the mediation of reason "the natural order divides the human race into social groups, nations or states, which are mutually independent in organization and in the direction of their internal life" (SP, 72).

But this division of mankind is not destined to break its essential unity; it is meant to enrich it by the sharing of communally achieved goods (SP, 43). Supposing the historical formation of political communities, these are subject to the same moral law as are individuals (PT, 80). The natural law of charity and justice evolves with the growth of social relationships. There is a "natural international law" (SP, 74) which regulates the development and activity of peoples as well as individuals, by which the equality and independence of each political community is morally guaranteed, from which further positive agreements and treaties between them draw their binding force, and on which the duties of mutual international aid are founded.

Thus, even as when two individuals meet the moral law imposes duties of mutual assistance in the pursuit of their common destiny, so also when two states come in contact they are bound to collaborate for the attainment of the common purpose for which they exist: the facilitation of human well-being. The natural law itself commands an international cooperation which embraces economic and cultural relations, exchanges of services and resources, diplomatic exchanges for mutual understanding, negotiations and conventions for the peaceful arbitration of international disputes, and special aid in times of distress.

Envisaged in this way, the international society is, analogously to the original community of the human family, an inorganic and moral society rather than a political one. And this is the factual situation. Despite the existence of more or less permanent organs and instruments of international cooperation, the great powers of the world do not submit themselves in every eventuality to a supreme authority in matters that touch on international relations. This is the further desired evolution of international society which, while also urged in previous papal statements (see note 1), is the culminating point of *Pacem in Terris*.

The encyclicals of Pope John treat of international society in both of these suppositions. *Mater et Magistra* and the third section of *Pacem in Terris* touch on the mutual rights and duties of states in the actual situation of imperfectly organized international relations, which "no longer correspond to the objective requirements of the universal common good." This is the situation of "peaceful coexistence." The fourth section of *Pacem in Terris* is a plea for the critically needed structural reorganization of international society involving "a public authority, having world-wide power and endowed with the proper means for the efficacious pursuit of its objectives." This would be a situation of organic unity.

The "new meaning" of the common good to which *Pacem in Terris* refers in this section is not found in the fact that there is now, in contrast with the past, a "universal" common good of all mankind, but in the fact that, in the present situation the common good of the lesser political units (the nation-states) is no longer viable without reference to and participation in that universal good. Whereas in past times the inevitable insularity of separated peoples may have allowed them to escape the impact (and led them to a forgetfulness) of human solidarity, today the close relations which modern science and technology have effected force them to work and live as one family. Human solidarity, always a moral imperative and Christian aspiration, has become an obtrusive necessity, which no one can escape, by reason of the actual interdependence of nations.

> The relations among nations everywhere have lately multiplied and increased under the impact of science and technology. In turn, their populations necessarily become more and more interdependent.

As a result, it can be said that contemporary problems of any importance, whatever their content may be—scientific, technical, economic, social, political, or cultural—today commonly present supranational and often global dimensions (MM, 200–201).

Science and technology are ambivalent factors in international relations. They have both unifying and divisive capabilities. The immediate result of scientific progress is a physical unification of states and peoples. Satellite systems have made world-wide communication nearly instantaneous, and distances have been dissolved by super-jets. Consequent on this unification, science and technology further open up a twofold possibility to the modern world: universal prosperity through the cooperative use of new techniques and new sources of energy, or human extinction through nuclear war. The possibility of both is acknowledged by the encyclicals (MM, 210; PT, 111, 130). But the encyclicals also stress that these are the choice of human wills.

Science and technology are tools. Their instrumental nature is mentioned several times by *Mater et Magistra* (e.g., 175, 246). They are not values which determine choice; they are the means to be used in the pursuit of values. The inversion of this order is deplored by the encyclical:

> We observe with sadness that many people in the economically advanced countries have no concern for a genuine hierarchy of values. These persons wholly neglect, put aside, or flatly deny the existence of spiritual values. Meanwhile they energetically pursue scientific and technological research and seek economic development. Material well being is in many instances their chief goal in life (MM, 176).

The naive optimism of seventeenth-century rationalism,

ridiculed today, was continued under the guise of evolutionary biologism in the last century and is still with us in the gadgetry-worship of modern technology. Technological improvement is taken as a sign of human progress. Civilization is thought to advance the faster we can move, by the more automation that can be introduced, and by the more problems that can be fed into a computer. And material well-being, which apparently limitless technology makes possible, becomes the supreme value of life. "It has been claimed . . . that in an era of scientific and technical triumphs, men can construct on their own a perfect civilization without God" (MM, 209).

More and more, however, even by the pragmatic test which the modern age accepts, the illusory nature of this optimism appears. Fears are expressed that man is being destroyed by his own machines. Humanism yields bit by bit to automatism, a trend that threatens to accelerate with the present educational emphasis on the practical. Peoples live in a community of fear as they realize that the gigantic forces placed at the disposal of technology can be used for destructive purposes, and that even "some uncontrollable and unexpected chance" can set off a conflagration with "fatal consequences for life on earth" (MM, 210; PT, 111).

Material well-being is a genuine part of human perfection, so important a part, in fact, that lasting and beneficial peace is impossible while glaring socio-economic inequalities persist between nations or classes (MM, 157). But it is not the supreme value of human life. Its value is instrumental. It provides the necessary means and condition which man's composite nature demands for a life of virtue.

Of itself, the material is a principle of division, not unity.

And therefore any human universalism founded merely on material prosperity is doomed to failure. Marx had a valid insight into the social nature of man and the creative role of united mankind. But his vision was internally vitiated by his promethean materialism and externally betrayed by its political implementation which finds symbolic expression in the Berlin Wall.

Hence ideologies which take into account only certain aspects of man, and these the less significant, fail as a cementing force of international relations (MM, 213). A more radical source of international unity must be sought in the realm of spiritual values, which, as spiritual, can be shared without being divided: those values are truth, justice, love, and freedom:

> Scientific competence, technical capacity, and professional experience, although necessary, are not of themselves sufficient to elevate the relationships of society to an order that is genuinely human, that is, to an order whose foundation is truth, whose measure and objective is justice, whose driving force is love, and whose method of attainment is freedom (PT, 149).

International unity, being human, must be a moral unity which is governed by the moral law. There is a solidarity of nations, which is a social projection of the solidarity of all men, and which is grounded on the same bedrock of the dignity of the human person. The equality of all men in virtue of their natural dignity is the reason for the unity of the human family. The same equality founds the equality of their political communities in the family of nations:

"All men are equal in their natural dignity. Consequently there are no political communities which are superior by nature, and none which are inferior by nature. All political communities are of equal natural dignity, since they are bodies whose membership is made up of these same human beings" (PT, 89).

Unabashedly, Pope John refers this dignity of the human person, as does the whole Christian tradition, to man's relation to God. The greatness of man depends on God, whose image he is, and it is foolish "to seek to exalt man's greatness by drying up the font from which his greatness springs and from which it is nourished, that is, by restraining and, if possible, checking his quest for God" (MM, 217). A moral order of justice and love cannot be built except on God. Cut off from God it disintegrates. Consequently,

> whatever the technical and economic progress, there will be neither justice nor peace in this world until men return to a sense of their dignity as creatures and sons of God. For He must be accepted as the initial and ultimate explanation of the existence of all his creatures. Man separated from God becomes inhuman to himself and to those about him, because the proper ordering of social relations presupposes the proper ordering of one's conscience to God, the source of all truth, justice, and love (MM, 215).

Mater et Magistra and *Pacem in Terris* go on to detail several demands which this natural solidarity of nations makes in the present international situation. They come under three headings: aid to be given to emerging and developing nations; disarmament and the establishment of peace; and (as a necessary means for the effective attainment of the other two) the establishment of a positive, juridically structured international society. These are specifications of natural international law, described by the encyclicals as demanded by "the solidarity which binds all men and makes them members, in a sense, of the same family" (MM, 157), by "justice and humanity," "equity and human kindness" (MM, 161), and by the "moral order itself" (PT, 137).

International aid is an abiding and perennial obligation of states. But it has an urgency today that can be neglected only at the peril of universal disaster. There is a crisis of international economic inequality which, because of the close interdependence of nations and because of the frustration of the legitimate expectations that all peoples have, can involve even the prosperous nations in ruins. The contrast between nations that are economically advanced and enjoy a high standard of living, and those in earlier stages of development which suffer from extreme poverty is therefore called "one of the most difficult problems facing the modern world" (MM, 157).

U Thant, Secretary General of the United Nations, has also pointed out the possible calamitous consequences of this inter-nation economic contrast, and, in his report to the twenty-first session of the General Assembly, added the warning that the gulf is widening. The rich industrialized nations are growing steadily richer, and the less developed countries are, at best, standing still, despite the existing programs for international aid and for economic development.

Indifference to this situation, which once might have been explained by ignorance or geographic separation, now has no excuse. "We are all equally responsible for the undernourished peoples" (PT, 158). Here the principles of social justice that govern the use of material goods is extended from individual to political communities. Property, whether individual or national, has a social aspect, and the stewardship of wealth rests on states as well as on private citizens.

> Everyone is aware that some countries have a surplus of consumer goods—especially farm produce—while in other lands large segments of the population suffer from hunger and want. Justice and humanity demand, then, that the rich come to the aid of the poor. To destroy or to squander goods that other people need for survival goes against all canons of equity and human kindness (MM, 161; see 153–155).

Analogously, too, international social justice demands the use of prudence in the aid that is given. The obligation is not merely to a "give away" program. Aid necessary to tide a people over an emergency may require a gratuitous distribution of national surpluses of consumer goods; but "emergency aid will not suffice to eliminate the permanent factors causing hunger and want." The furnishing of capital, technical assistance, education, and professional training must be included in the long range aid which the primitive nature of developing economies requires (MM, 163–165). Disproportions between manpower and available land or capital call for collaboration between peoples to facilitate "the circulation from one to the other of capital, goods, and manpower" (PT, 101). Immigration policies should be liberalized as much as possible (PT, 107).

A further and more significant feature of Pope John's development of the obligation of international aid is his insistence on the spiritual qualities which must characterize it. It must be founded on truth, measured by justice, inspired by love, and accomplished in freedom. These are the values, as has been said, which alone can fashion human community, and without which material prosperity remains merely a source of contention.

If international cooperation and aid are to measure up to the standard of these values in the contemporary scene, modifications must be made in certain contemporary attitudes and practices. The acknowledgment of the equality of all states, founded on the equal human dignity of their members, is the first requisite (PT, 86–89).

Differences in levels of culture, civilization, or economic development are not justifications for the dominance of one state over others. Every trace of racism must be eliminated. The pose of essential superiority assumed by the technologically more advanced nations must be abandoned. The use of international propaganda and international defamation, made possible by modern media of social communication, must be discarded as a perversion of a means of mutual knowledge and understanding (PT, 90). Nothing must interfere with the right of every state to existence, to self-development and the means to its attainment, and to be the one primarily responsible for this self-development (PT, 92).

As a consequence, international aid must be characterized by political disinterestedness. The freedom and individuality of all peoples and the rich human values their various geniuses contribute to universal well-being must be respected. Help given to less developed nations must not be distorted into a means of extending spheres of interest or exporting ideologies, nor must it be conditioned by the imposition of the helper's way of life. Such assistance "must be labeled explicitly as an effort to introduce a new form of colonialism, which, however cleverly disguised, would be only a repetition of that old, outdated type from which many people have recently escaped" (MM, 169–174; PT, 120).

The purpose of international aid is to help under-developed nations to reach that social and economic maturity which enables them to fulfill their internal and external responsibilities. They are themselves to be "the principal artisans in the promotion of their own economic development and social progress" (PT, 123). They have the further obligation of contributing "on a basis of equality," to the prosperity of the world community. As in the economic community of the single nation, so in the international community of all nations, the performance of duty as well as the enjoyment of rights is a part of truly human order (PT, 91). Interference with the freedom of poorer nations would make both impossible.

Obviously connected with the problem of international aid is Pope John's second topic of situational international concern, namely, that of disarmament and the establishment of peace. *Pacem in Terris* notes this connection:

> It is with deep sorrow that we note the enormous stocks of armaments that have been and still are being made in the more economically developed countries with a vast outlay of intellectual and economic resources. And so it happens that, while the people of these countries are loaded with heavy burdens, other countries as a result are deprived of the collaboration they need in order to make economic and social progress (PT, 109).

Others, too, have pointed to the interconnection of these two problems: "I believe that it is a violation of natural law for half the people of the world to live in misery, in abject poverty, without hope for the future, while the affluent nations spend on militarism a sum of money equal to the entire income of this miserable half of the world's people."[2]

But disarmament, today, is more than a condition for

international collaboration. It is an indispensable condition for universal survival, for the modern tools of war can be "tools for the annihilation of the human race" (MM, 210).

Modern armamentation is not merely a legitimate provision of adequate defense. It has become a competitive arms race with a constantly spiraling production of weapons of war. Equality in destructive power is looked upon as the only effective preservative of peace (PT, 109–118). The world is sitting not on an outmoded powder keg but on a nuclear warhead which can be touched off, even accidentally, by the push of a button.

The result of this mad process is not the tranquility of order but the reign of universal fear. And its remedy must be the substitution of reason for madness. The fundamental principle on which present-day peace depends—equality of arms—must be replaced by another—mutual trust (PT, 113). War in this atomic age cannot be used as an instrument of justice (PT, 127). In any case or time, "relations between states, as between individuals, should be regulated, not by the force of arms, but by the light of reason, by the rule, that is, of truth, of justice, and of active and sincere co-operation." But today there is no alternative to extinction but this rule of reason. Progressive disarmament, equal (not unilateral)[3] and simultaneous reduction of stockpiles which is complete and thorough, are modern determinations of the natural law itself:

> Justice, right reason, and humanity, therefore, urgently demand that the arms race should cease; that stockpiles which exist in various countries should be reduced equally and simultaneously by the parties concerned; that nuclear weapons should be banned; and that a general agreement should eventually be reached about progressive disarmament and an effective method of control (PT, 112).

It is precisely because of the impossiblity of achieving these objectives of effective international cooperation and especially world security and peace, as long as (to use the expression of Barbara Ward)[4] "the final decisions lie with the bargain makers at the national level," that Pope John in the fourth section of *Pacem in Terris* makes the appeal for the establishment of a politically organized international society.

In times past one may have been justified, as *Pacem in Terris* says (No. 133), in feeling that provision for the universal common good could be made through what the encyclical calls "normal" channels of diplomatic relations, top level meetings, conventions or treaties between nations which are not subject to any supranational authority.

This is no longer the situation. The world has become one in a sense that never before was true. National economies are integral parts of the one world economy. The prosperity and development of any political community is "a reflection and component part of the prosperity and development of all the other political communities" (PT, 131). The dispersion of authority through autonomous political groups, which makes international cooperation dependent today on the fluctuating and rescindable bargaining of these groups, no longer corresponds to this factual unity and interdependence. Even the best of good will and enterprise on the part of statesmen fail to meet the objective requirements of the universal common good because of this structural defect (PT, 134–135).

"There exists an intrinsic connection between the common good on the one hand and the structures and functions of public authority on the other" (PT, 136). As has been said, the whole reason and, therefore, the measure of authority, is the attainment of the common good. Consequently, as the common good increases in complexity and extent the structure of authority also must change. The organs through which it "is institutionalized, becomes operative and pursues its end" must be accommodated to the new complexity and extent.

From these considerations *Pacem in Terris* concludes to the necessity today of public authorities endowed with the power and structure and means which enable them to act in an effective manner on a world-wide basis. "The moral order itself, therefore, demands that such a form of public authority be established" (PT, 137).

The necessity of a supreme international authority is especially evident as regards international security and world peace. Here the danger is particularly grave and the solution difficult to the point of discouragement, as experience shows. Increased tension is the one palpable result of negotiations between states that continue to test the destructive power of nuclear weapons and to build anti-missile missiles at the very time they confer.

Balance of power is an anachronistic mechanism of peace, which even in the nineteenth century was a dubious preventive of slow mobilization for war, but which, today, is nothing but a generator of fear which destroys hope of collaboration. For today's power is that of total incineration which is already mobilized for instant delivery. Even as the attempt to fit legitimate democracy into a liberalistic scheme of society runs into totalitarianism, so the attempt to fit the potentially unifying forces of modern science and technology into a world of nationalism must end in conflict. International control of the dogs of war and the obligatory settlement of international disputes by an authority which all nations accept are the only insurance of world peace. War cannot be left to the decision of sensitive nations subject to the irritants which close neighbors experience.

The concept of a "supranational or world-wide authority" (PT, 138) is bound to disturb the cherished notions of those who confuse patriotism with chauvinism, or who see a communist plot in every suggestion of diminishing national sovereignty. Yet it is the clear teaching of the encyclical. "National sovereignty" is a much abused and misunderstood term. The implications it has historically acquired, of complete autonomy and independence, have led Maritain to suggest that we must get rid of the word and concept of sovereignty in political philosophy.[5]

Catholic social teaching does not call for this complete abandonment of the term, as is evident from the fact that Pius XII speaks of the "equal right to its own sovereignty" which every state retains even under effective international authority.[6] It must, however, be rid of the baneful isolationist connotation with which it was encrusted in a world in which there was no alternative to self-protection other than the non-aggression pacts of independent states.

Sovereignty implies independence in government, but not unlimited or absolute independence. It is the independence that states have to run their own internal affairs and to fulfill their external obligations without interference. It is therefore relative, being internally limited by the rights of the members of the political community, and externally limited by the progressive requirements of the international common good. In urging the specific limitation of national sovereignty which consists in subordination to an international authority, *Pacem in Terris* is merely applying a traditional doctrine of limitation to the world situation of today. The tradition itself is constant.

The "self-sufficiency" which natural law philosophy has predicated of the "perfect" civil society never signified complete independence. In St. Thomas,[7] the "perfection" of political communities is graded: a city is a perfect community, but a province is more perfect. Similarly, Suarez[8] teaches that "perfect" societies can be dependent societies, as cities within a kingdom, and that no state is so individually self-sufficient that it does not need the aid and society of others. A more modern exposition of the tradition, the *Code de Morale Internationale*,[9] places the state's claim to national independence and perfection in its capacity to maintain order and peace within its own boundaries rather than in its complete autarky. And Pius XII lays an immediate foundation for the plea of *Pacem in Terris* when he declares that

> the idea which credits the state with unlimited authority ... breaks the unity of supernational society ... no one can fail to see how the claim of absolute autonomy for the state stands in open opposition to the natural law that is inherent in man ... and therefore leaves the stability of international relations at the mercy of the will of rulers, while it destroys the possibility of true union and fruitful collaboration directed to the common good (SP, 71, 73).

Recognition of the need to curtail national sovereignty is growing, as is clear from the statements of many of the scholars and statesmen who convened in New York City, in February, 1965, to discuss the practical implications of *Pacem in Terris*. Arnold Toynbee, for instance, remarks:

> I do not believe that mere coexistence is going to be possible for much longer in the new kind of world into which we have now moved.... The accelerating pace of technological advance is making it increasingly difficult to solve our problems on any scale short of a world-wide one.... I believe

these jobs can be dealt with only by world authorities with effective power to override the national governments ... it is to the mutual interest of the nations to subordinate their national sovereignty to world authority. This is the only condition on which the nations can survive in the atomic age.[10]

Legitimate national sovereignty is safeguarded in the organized world community through the application of the principle of subsidiarity. *Pacem in Terris* extends this principle from the national to the international community. Subsidiarity, which *Quadragesimo Anno* called the fundamental principle of social philosophy and explained so lucidly in the context of the nation state, is applied by Pope John to international society (PT, 140). State sovereignty is similar to individual liberty in a world-wide projection of the problem of the reconciliation of liberty and authority.

Just as the subsidiary character of state authority leaves individuals and families and private associations free to develop themselves in an exercise of personal responsibility, so also the same subsidiary nature of world authority leaves the separate states the independence that belongs to them in the performance of their specific function. The public authority of the world community, therefore, does not take the place of the authority of the individual political communities. It is exercised over the states themselves which retain their own proper good, and which still have the right and duty of regulating the activities and assuring the security and rights of their citizens. As long as the individual states fulfill this mission the world authority cannot interfere. "On the contrary, its purpose is to create, on a world basis, an environment in which the public authorities of each political community, its citizens and intermediate associations, can carry out their tasks, fulfill their duties, and exercise their rights with greater security" (PT, 141).

According to the principle of subsidiarity, the proper purpose of the world authority is to "tackle and solve problems of an economic, social, political, or cultural character which are posed by the common good" and which because of their vastness, complexity, and urgency "the public authorities of the individual states are not in a position to tackle with any hope of a positive solution" (PT, 140). World authority can take direct action in state affairs, again according to the principle of subsidiarity, only "when required," that is, when the lesser political units fail in their task. Such a case might be the protection of basic human rights against tyranny, for "the public authority of the world community, too, must have as its fundamental objective the recognition, respect, safeguarding, and promotion of the rights of the human person" (PT, 139).

Legitimate national independence and equality point to another facet of the world authority which *Pacem in Terris* describes. It must be set up by common accord and not imposed by force (PT, 138).

Participation of citizens in the determination of their government, as has been said, is in keeping with their dignity as human persons. Less cannot be said of the creation of an international authority by their political communities. These too enjoy a dignity and equality which is rooted in human personality, no matter what their differences may be in economic development or military might (PT, 89). And therefore "they are right in not easily yielding in obedience to an authority imposed by force, or to an authority in whose creation they had no part or to which they themselves did not decide to submit by conscious and free choice" (PT, 138).

An equally important and perhaps more pragmatic reason for this common accord is that of the effectiveness of world-wide authority (PT, 138). Interior conviction and trust are conditions of the stability of political institutions and of their effective operation. That is why trust must replace the principle of fear on which our present peace is built. Experience proves that freedom, not force, is the condition of fruitful cooperation. All dictatorships eventually learn this truth. Conviction, trust, and freedom are eliminated in a world order forcibly imposed.

Pope John does not suggest that this necessary organization of international society is going to be realized immediately. "It must be borne in mind that to proceed gradually is the law of life in all its expressions. Therefore, in human institutions, too, it is not possible to renovate for the better except by working from within them gradually" (PT, 162).

A social order founded on truth, built according to justice, vivified and integrated by charity, and put into practice in freedom remains to be constructed. But it is not, in the thinking of Pope John, a hopeless task. The optimism that pervades *Mater et Magistra* and *Pacem in Terris* is founded on two things: faith in the help of the Prince of Peace, and the aspiration shared by "all men of good will" to the consolidation of peace in the world (PT, 166, 168).

> There is reason to hope, however, that by meeting and negotiation men may come to discover better the bonds—deriving from the human nature which they have in common—that unite them, and that they may learn also that one of the most profound requirements of their common nature is this: that between them and their respective peoples it is not fear which should reign but love, a love which tends to express itself in a collaboration that is loyal, manifold in form, and productive of many benefits (PT, 129).

CHAPTER SEVEN

EVERY MAN A BROTHER

The first papal encyclical of the modern international era was perhaps Pius XII's *The Unity of Human Society* (1939). Written at a time when the promises and dangers of growing international unity were only dimly seen, it had as its theme universal brotherhood, the solidarity of the human family. Almost 30 years later, the encyclical of Paul VI, *Populorum Progressio*, which summarizes the teaching of the social encyclicals on international life, stresses the same theme: every man a brother.

In the time between these encyclicals, as John XXIII emphasized (see chapter six), science and technology had created an even more closely-knit international community. This development has underlined the truth of human solidarity, and made the moral imperative of universal love more insistent and detailed. It has further served to highlight the urgency of the situation of international misery and want in the midst of plenty. "The world is sick," Paul declares (PP, 66), but the sickness, in his diagnosis, does not consist basically in the pitiable hunger or misery of so many peoples and nations. These are but symptoms; the real illness lies "in the lack of brotherhood between individuals and peoples" (PP, 66).

Brotherhood and solidarity are therefore the constantly repeated theme of Paul's solemn appeal. The anguished cry of hungry peoples is a "brother's cry for help" (PP, 3); "man must meet man, nation meet nation, as brothers and sisters" (PP, 43); the duty of international aid stems "from a brotherhood that is at once human and supernatural" (PP, 44); "no one can remain indifferent to the lot of his brother" (PP, 74). It is only through solidarity in action that the aspirations of man can be realized: "Solidarity in action at this turning point in human history is a matter of urgency" (PP, 1).

This last statement is a capsule repetition of the warning of John XXIII. As has been said (chapter six), the message of *Pacem in Terris* especially is the "new meaning of the common good." No problem or crisis or interest can any longer be the insular concern of any individual political community. Both the realization of the promises of modern technology as well as the very preservation of mankind in the face of its threats demand the effective organization of international society. Solidarity in action is a matter of urgency.

As these considerations suggest, the doctrine of *Populorum Progressio* is not new. It is incorporated (PP, 2) into the tradition of the great social encyclicals of Leo XIII, Pius XI and John XXIII which have been discussed in the preceding chapters. It calls for the implementation of their social teaching especially in its international dimension, and summarizes that teaching's pertinent points. It is an urgent repetition of the admonition of John XXIII that the social question, the common subject of the social encyclicals, has become world wide (PP, 3). It reiterates the "anguished appeal" of John XXIII (PP, 46) for international social justice.

Pope Paul gives a new nuance to this tradition by organizing it around the idea of a "true" and "complete humanism" (PP, 42). He seems to be accepting the challenge of those who locate the religion of today in the cultivation of the secular city, by pointing out the fact that the social teaching of traditional Christianity is the teaching of authentic human fulfillment; its aim is "the construction of a more human world" (PP, 54). The dimensions of this authentic humanism remain to be examined. But first, and by way of necessary digression, let it be said that the event has proved the necessity of this summary review of papal social teaching by Paul. The reception accorded to *Populorum Progressio* in certain circles makes it abundantly, even frighteningly, clear that the teaching of the earlier social encyclicals has not been properly understood.

Time magazine (April 7, 1967), for instance, speaks of a considerable shift to the left of previous papal encyclicals in *Populorum Progressio's* criticism of private property. In contrast to Leo's assertion of the inviolability of private property, and John's defense of it as a natural right, Paul's declaration of the limitation of property rights is highlighted, with the clear implication, contained in *Time's* phrase "on the other hand," that Paul had deserted the position of his predecessors. Enough has perhaps been said on this subject in Chapter Two of the present work to repudiate the idea that Paul "shifts considerably to the left." If one thing is crystal clear in the Church's tradition of the inviolable, natural right of private ownership, it is its insistence on the social limitations and restrictions of that right. The stewardship of wealth, the social responsibility of property, the duty of the social use of superfluous goods, the social aspect of ownership as it concerns the common good—these are all emphasized by Leo, Pius, and John as well as by Paul. They are derived, as John has written, from the very considerations that justify ownership itself (MM, 120).

Even the seemingly radical suggestion, by which Pope Paul exemplifies the conditioned nature of the right of property, of the expropriation of certain landed estates that impede the general prosperity (PP, 24) was proposed as far back as 1927 (see *A Code of Social Principles*, no. 98, prepared by the International Union of Social Studies, 3rd edition, Oxford, 1948), and repeated by the Second Vatican Council ("The Church in the Modern World," No. 71, in Documents of Vatican II, p. 281). There is no considerable shift to the left here.

Nor is the criticism that *Populorum Progressio* reflects the economic perspective of another time justified. Paul's encyclical is not a Quixotic tilting "which virtually ignored the fact that old style *laissez-faire* capitalism is about as dead as *Das Kapital*." Paul was very well aware of the statement made by Pius XII in 1931 that Leo XIII had boldly broken through the principles of the old liberalism which were even then "tottering" (QA, 27); he accepted the tremendous social and economic changes, which had been enumerated by John XXIII, of social security and insurance systems, welfare benefits, union power and activity, increased government control of economic affairs—all of which marked the passing of *laissez-faire* capitalism.

Laissez-faire capitalism as a system is dead; but *laissez-faire* capitalists are not. The short-sighted selfishness, the greed and avarice which Pope Paul calls "the most evident form of moral underdevelopment" for both nations and individuals (PP, 19), and which the system once dignified by the term "profit motive," are still potent factors in the economic life of many individuals and nations.

Much less does Paul condemn capitalism or industrialism. Rather he praises them for their evident benefits, their "irreplaceable contribution" to development (PP, 26). He would not abolish the competitive market (PP, 61), but insists that competition must be kept within the limits that humanity and social justice demand. In the matter of capitalism and competition he is but repeating the distinctions made by Pope Puis XI between the system of capitalism in itself, which is not to be condemned, and the perversion of that system through callous selfishness (QA, 101), and again, between fair competition which is beneficial, and unfettered competition which can never be the supreme guide of economic activity (QA, 85).

It is only a guilty sensitivity which could see in *Populorum Progressio* a radical and blunt attack on capitalism, and detect Marxian overtones in the allegedly vague and mild warnings, which by contrast, are given against systems that are based on a materialistic and atheistic philosophy.

Far from being vague and mild, the whole message of *Populorum Progressio* is a condemnation of materialism and atheism wherever they are found, for the "humanism" for which it pleads is precisely that which is "open to the values of the spirit and to God who is their source" (PP, 42). It is, in fact, a humanism in which the natural enrichment of man is ordered to a further "transcendent humanism," a "new fulfillment" wherein man finds "his greatest possible perfection" in supernatural union with Christ (PP, 16).

The "development" (*progressio*) of which Paul speaks means "complete fulfillment" (PP, 1). Development is the response to the vocation of every life whereby the special aptitudes of each are brought to fruition and each man grows in humanity and becomes more a person (PP, 15). It is equivalated by the encyclical itself with "complete humanism" (PP, 42).

This "complete humanism" of *Populorum Progressio* is three-dimensional, reaching, as it does, to the height of God, to the depth of the spirituality of man, and to the outer extremities of all mankind. "Development . . . in order to be authentic . . . must be complete, integral; that is, it has to promote the good of every man and of the whole man" (PP, 14). One recalls, in this reference to the "whole man," the warning of John XXIII against those who would root a social order in false ideologies which take into consideration "only certain aspects of man and these the less significant" (MM, 213).

The "whole man" is fundamentally and essentially religious. Human fulfillment is not an arbitrarily chosen ideal. Man, like the whole of creation, of which he is a part, is ordered to God the Creator, with this difference that man's orientation can be freely accepted. He fulfills himself in its acceptance (PP, 16). Consequently "there is no true humanism but that which is open to the Absolute and is conscious of a vocation which gives human life its true meaning" (PP, 42). There can be no authentic self-realization without a religious perspective.

Paul tersely stresses the impact of this religious dimension of man on the cultivation of the secular city: "An isolated humanism is an inhuman humanism" (PP, 42). Apart from God man is no longer truly man. The dignity of man as a person resides in the inviolable image of God which each one is. It was this personal dignity which, as has been said (chapter one, page 6), John XXIII made the root of all true human order.

How fragile human dignity becomes when deprived of its religious dimension is the lesson that every form of materialism teaches. *Mater et Magistra* therefore called that modern error most fundamental which considered the "religious instinct of the human soul . . . an obstacle to human progress" (MM, 214). "Whatever the technical and economic progress, there will be neither justice nor peace in this world until men return to a sense of their dignity as creatures and sons of God. For He must be accepted as the initial and ultimate explanation of the existence of all His creatures. Man separated from God becomes inhuman to himself and to those about him" (MM, 215). Unless the Lord build the city—the secular city—they labor in vain who build it. "True, man can organise the world apart from God, but 'without God man can organise it in the end only to man's detriment' " (PP, 42). The world is rightly organized, making authentic human development possible, only when it "will enable modern man to find himself anew by embracing the higher values of love, friendship, of prayer and contemplation" (PP, 20).

Quite evidently this development includes more than the mere economic development of the emerging nations. It is the self-fulfillment which is for "each and all"—economically advanced or not—"the transition from less human conditions to those which are more human" (PP, 20). Less human conditions can be found in cultured as well as in primitive people; underdevelopment can be moral as well as physical.

The encyclical is not impractically idealistic. This call to embrace the "higher values of love" is also a call to express that love in the relief of hunger and misery (PP, 74), in the sharing of material goods (PP, 23, 49), and in the elimination of the scandal of glaring inequalities (PP, 9). In fact, it is by the neglect of these elementally human offices that "flourishing civilizations . . . selfishly wrapped up in themselves . . . could easily place their highest values in jeopardy" (PP, 49). Love is proved by deeds.

Populorum Progressio is very much down to earth. Before all else, human fulfillment requires the removal of "living and working conditions unworthy of the human person" (PP, 9). "Too many are suffering" (29), "whole continents are ravished by hunger, countless numbers of children are undernourished, so that many of them die in infancy, while the physical growth and mental development of many others are retarded and as a result whole regions are condemned to the most depressing despondency" (PP, 45). "Brothers are still buried in wretchedness and victims of insecurity, slaves of ignorance" (PP, 74); "the poor nations remain poor, while the rich ones become still richer" (PP, 57). The injustice of the situation cries to heaven (PP, 30). "We must make haste" (PP, 29) because "the very life of poor nations, civil peace in developing countries, and world peace itself are at stake" (PP, 55).

Thus, in so many ways does Paul call for the removal of economic and social injustice as the initial step in the realization of human fulfillment. But, in just so many ways, he emphasizes that this is only an initial step in a program of complete humanism. "Development cannot be limited to mere economic growth . . . it has to promote the good . . . of the whole man" (PP, 14). "Increased possession is not the ultimate goal of nations or individuals . . . the exclusive pursuit of possessions [thus] becomes an obstacle to individual fulfilment and to man's true greatness" (PP, 19). "It is not sufficient to promote technology to render the world a more human place in which to live" (PP, 34). Dialogue between peoples is necessary to determine the needs of international cooperation, but it must be "a dialogue based on man, and not on commodities or technical skills," which will guarantee "not merely economic but human development" (PP, 73).

Economic fulfillment is basic, but it is not total human fulfillment. Herein is the depth of the complete humanism which *Populorum Progressio* proposes and which is summed up in perhaps the key paragraph of the encyclical:

> It is not just a matter of eliminating hunger, nor even of reducing poverty. The struggle against destitution, though urgent and necessary, is not enough. It is a question, rather, of building a world where every man, no matter what his race, religion, or nationality, can live a fully human life, freed from servitude imposed on him by other men or by natural forces over which he has not sufficient control; a world where freedom is not an empty word and where the poor man Lazarus can sit down at the same table with the rich man. This demands great generosity, much sacrifice and unceasing effort on the part of the rich man (PP, 47).

Although the transition from less human conditions envisages particularly "those people who are striving to escape from hunger, misery, endemic diseases, and ignorance—those who are looking for a wider share in the benefits of civilization" (PP, 1)—nevertheless it is not applied exclusively to these so-called emerging or economically underdeveloped nations. It encompasses all nations and peoples. All are still striving for human fulfillment.

Humanistic fulfillment is as dynamic as human life. And therefore the materially developed nations have not reached, and never will reach, a place of static perfection which they can enjoy with narcissistic complacency. They are, in fact, humanly fulfilled only in the fulfillment of all peoples, for true humanism is realized only in solidarity.

One of the most striking features of *Populorum Progressio* is its continual insistence on this point. Again and again the idea is repeated in a variety of expressions that the fulfillment of all is a condition of the fulfillment of each (e.g. PP, 5, 14, 17, 20, 42, 43, 65). And, consequently, the humanism which the encyclical proposes is not a sterile speculative analysis but a fruitful principle which issues in such practical conclusions as the establishment of a world fund for the relief of the destitute (PP, 51), international subsidies and price supports to effect a balance of trade and promote the growth of industries (PP, 56–62), a readiness to pay higher taxes for intensified international development (47).

Complete self-development of individuals or of peoples is impossible in isolation. Man achieves his human perfection only in the communication of goods (see chapter three). This has always been the clear message of the social encyclicals, but Paul gives that message a new and rather startling formulation: "There can be no progress towards the complete development of man without the simultaneous development of all humanity in the spirit of solidarity" (PP, 43).

The "oneness" or solidarity of mankind is such that no man or nation can attain human fulfillment as long as the fulfillment of any is neglected. There is an identity of all by reason of which the fate of one is the fate of all—not merely in the evident possibility of universal atomic destruction, but in the actuality of self-realization. It is in the light of this truth that nationalism, which together with racism is singled out as an obstacle to human unity, is criticized not precisely for isolating people from others (which it certainly does) but for isolating them "from their own good" (PP, 62); the good of the "whole man" includes the good of "every man."

Nations are reminded that "fulness of development" is a communal responsibility (PP, 17); that technically competent nations do not "enjoy a monopoly of valuable elements" (PP, 72); that there is a plurality of cultures and civilizations all contributing to human enrichment and "many nations poorer in economic goods are quite rich in wisdom and able to offer noteworthy advantages to others" (PP, 40); that "a more human world" supposes "an effective and mutual sharing, carried out with equal dignity on either side" (PP, 54).

This communal pursuit of human fulfillment, as *Populorum Progressio* points out, places a special duty of brotherhood on the "better-off nations" (PP, 44). The strong must help the weak; this is the essence of brotherhood. But the purpose of this aid is not to perpetuate a state of dependence, even though the subsistence of all is thereby assured. Among the "wrongs to human dignity" which *Populorum Progressio* stigmatizes is the situation wherein "whole populations destitute of necessities live in a state of dependence barring them from all initiative and responsibility" (PP, 30). The purpose of aid "is not just a matter of eliminating hunger . . . but building a world where every man can live a fully human life" (PP, 47)—and a fully human life means the realization of the higher values of the spirit.

"Man is only truly man in as far as, master of his own acts and judge of their worth, he is author of his own advancement, in keeping with the nature which was given to him by his Creator and whose possibilities and exigencies he himself freely assumes" (PP, 34). This individual human fulfillment finds its counterpart in the life of peoples who are to "become the artisans of their destiny" (PP, 65). This is the goal of international collaboration.

Just as the exercise of responsibility, as has been said (see chapter four), is an index of personal dignity for the working man, and incorporates him into a humanized economic community, so the exercise of responsibility in the world of international affairs is the index of human fulfillment on the level of national life, and integrates the nation in the larger life of humanity. The goal of complete humanism is that every man and people may be able to share in and exercise responsibility for all areas of human life.

The duties of the more prosperous nations to the poorer, indicated in detail by *Populorum Progressio*, correspond to this idea of a growth from dependence to responsible self-fulfillment. They take on a threefold aspect: the duty of human solidarity—the aid that the rich nations must give to developing countries; the duty of social justice—the rectification of inequitable trade relations between powerful nations and weak nations; the duty of universal charity—the effort to bring about a world that is more human towards all men, where all will be able to give and receive, without one group making progress at the expense of others (PP, 44).

The duty of human solidarity, of aid, repeats the teaching of the previous social encyclicals on the use of superfluous wealth, and recalls again the teaching of John XXIII that the duties of the stewardship of wealth extend to nations (MM, 157–158). "We must repeat once more that the super-fluous wealth of rich countries should be placed at the service of poor nations" (PP, 49).

> When so many people are hungry, when so many families suffer from destitution, when so many remain steeped in ignorance, when so many schools, hospitals, and homes worthy of the name remain to be built, all public and private squandering of wealth, all expenditures prompted by motives of national or personal ostentation, every exhausting armaments race, becomes an intolerable scandal (PP, 53).

These words and others just as sharp are not merely emotional rhetoric; they do not call for a sentimental response whose effectiveness is dissipated in emotionally inspired flurries of ill considered hand-outs. There is a notable hard-headedness in the proposals of the encyclical. The stewardship of wealth is a work of prudence.

For one thing, an examination of conscience is suggested by Paul which is as disturbing as it is simple and direct.

> Let each one examine his conscience, a conscience that conveys a new message for our times. Is he prepared to support out of his own pocket works and undertakings organised in favor of the most destitute? Is he ready to pay higher taxes so that the public authorities can intensify their efforts in favor of development? Is he ready to pay a higher price for imported goods so that the producer may be more justly rewarded? Or to leave his country, if necessary and if he is young, in order to assist in this development of the young nations? (PP, 47).

Again it is stressed that the effectiveness of international aid calls for concerted planning (PP, 50). Between those who contribute wealth and those who benefit a dialogue is absolutely necessary to make an assessment of the necessary contributions in terms of available wealth, on one hand, and real needs, on the other (PP, 54). And cynical critics of foreign aid programs will be disappointed in finding their image of an international Polyanna destroyed in the words: "Guarantees could be given to those who provide the capital that it will be put to use according to an agreed plan and with a reasonable measure of efficiency, since there is no question of encouraging parasites or the indolent" (PP, 54).

The second duty—"the duty of social justice—the rectification of inequitable trade relations"—is a duty of helping the growing nations to help themselves rather than a duty of outright aid. Efforts to assist developing nations on a financial and technical basis must not be nullified by trade relations which further impoverish the weaker nations (PP, 56).

In this context we see again the frequently noted evolution in continuity of the social encyclicals. Paul invokes the teaching of Leo XIII on the justice of the wage contract and extends it to "international contracts" (PP, 59). *Rerum Novarum* had condemned complete freedom of contract, or rather that false and one-sided "freedom" which selfish individualism defended in the name of economic law but which was nothing but economic dictatorship. "Let . . . worker and employer . . . enter freely into agreements . . . yet there is always underlying such agreements an element of natural justice, one greater and more ancient than the free consent of contracting parties. . . . If, compelled by necessity . . . a worker accept a harder condition, which although against his will he must accept because the employer or contractor imposes it, he certainly submits to force against which justice cries out in protest" (RN, 63).

Populorum Progressio bases its plea for some sort of international subsidies and price support, established through international agreements (PP, 61) on the same grounds: the rule of free agreement must be subservient to the demands of the more fundamental natural law (PP, 59). Here "the fundamental principle of liberalism, as the rule for commercial exchange ... is questioned" (PP, 58). What is true of the wage contract for individuals is also true of international contracts. "Freedom of trade is fair only if it is subject to the demands of social justice" (PP, 59). "In trade between developed and underdeveloped economies, conditions are too disparate and the degrees of genuine freedom available too unequal. In order that international trade be human and moral, social justice requires that it restore to the participants a certain equality of opportunity" (PP, 61).

The third duty which "is the concern especially of better-off nations" is that of "universal charity—the effort to bring about a world which is more human to all men, where all will be able to give and receive" (PP, 44). Here it is a question of the goal which international aid must attain: the goal of "complete humanism."

Poorer nations and their members are to be accepted, warmly welcomed, and treated as equals. Condescension has no place in brotherhood and is soon recognized with resentment (PP, 71). Much less can exploitation be reconciled with the social sensitivity which brotherhood implies (PP, 70). Universal charity is incompatible with the idea of one group making progress at the expense of another (PP, 44).

Here we find repeated the notion of international equality which John XXIII insisted upon, and which he based on the fact that all nations are made up of equal human persons (see chapter six). All genuinely human relations, international as well as personal, must "recognize in man his true value" (PP, 71). Nations must realize that, whatever their technical competence and superiority, they are still enriched by the contributions of other cultures and other civilizations (PP, 72–73).

It is precisely in this mutuality of contributions that peoples take their place in a "more human world." A "complete humanism" is one that allows all peoples to be the artisans of their own destiny and to take their responsible place in mutual collaboration for the good of all (PP, 65). "The younger or weaker nations ask to assume their active part in the construction of a better world, one which shows deeper respect for the rights and vocation of the individual. This is a legitimate appeal; everyone should hear it and respond to it" (PP, 65).

The complaint is not uncommon that "the greatest decisions affecting man's future are being made in the sphere of the secular; and Christianity does not seem to be there." *Populorum Progressio*, as has been suggested, would almost seem to be a formal answer to this complaint. Empathy for contemporary secular man, for the world and its concerns, characterizes the encyclical. "Authentic human development" is its thematic summary of Christian social teaching.

Robert McAfee Brown, commenting (*Commonweal*, May 19, 1967) on the ecumenical impact of the encyclical in this context, observes:

> *Populorum Progressio* is not putting on the brakes, nor is it simply repeating the ideas of *Rerum Novarum, Quadragesimo Anno, Mater et Magistra*, and *Pacem in Terris*. It picks up on the ideas in those encyclicals, to be sure, but it does not stand

still. . . . On the front of common concern for mankind, Pope Paul is taking vigorous and dynamic leadership, and . . . in this increasingly central part of the ecumenical task, non-Catholics will have to scramble to keep up with him. His concerns here can be symbolized by what is probably the most brilliant line of the entire encyclical: "The new name for peace is development."

NOTES

CHAPTER ONE

1. *The Documents of Vatican II*, ed. Walter M. Abbott, S.J. (paper ed., New York, 1966), p. 3.

2. *Acta Apostolicae Sedis*, v. 43 (Feb. 28, 1951), p. 169.

3. Christmas Message, 1952. (AAS, 45 [1953]), p. 35.

4. *Pattern for Peace*, H. W. Flannery (Westminster, Md., 1962), pp. 253 ff.

CHAPTER TWO

1. "The Church Today," in *The Documents of Vatican II*, no. 71.

2. *De Regimine Principum* (Taurini, 1924), Bk. I, c. 15.

3. Adam Smith, *The Wealth of Nations*, in vols. 16, 17, 18, *A Library of Universal Literature* (New York, 1901), Bk. IV, c. 9.

4. *Ibid.*, Bk. IV, c. 2.

5. *Ibid.*, Bk. IV, c. 9; Bk. V, c. 1, part II.

6. Karl Marx, *The Communist Manifesto*, in *Capital, The Communist Manifesto and Other Writings*, ed. Max Eastman (New York, 1932), p. 337.

7. Marx, *Economic and Philosophical Manuscripts of 1844*, in *Marx's Concept of Man* by Erich Fromm (New York, 1961), pp. 101, 137.

8. *Ibid.*, p. 139.

9. Frederick Engels, *Socialism Utopian and Scientific* (New York, 1935), p. 16.

10. Marx, *Critique of Political Economy*, in *Capital, The Communist Manifesto*, etc., pp. 10–11.

11. *The Communist Manifesto*, p. 322; also *Manuscripts of 1844*, p. 127.

12. A remarkable illustration of the affinity between liberalism and communism is found in Adam Smith's explanation of the origin and purpose of the state. It could have been written by Marx. Cf. *Wealth of Nations*, Bk. V, c. 1.

13. W. P. Drummond, S.J., *Social Justice* (Milwaukee, 1955), p. 55.

14. "The Church Today," no. 30.

15. See A. A. Berle and G. C. Means, *The Modern Corporation and Private Property* (New York, 1932); also A. A. Berle, *Power without Property* (New York, 1959).

16. "The Church Today," no. 71, note 223.

17. *Ibid.*, no. 69.

18. Hom. in Luc., "Destruam," art 2 (Migne, P.G., 31, 263).

19. Hom. 20 in Ev. (Migne, P.L., 76, 1165).

20. In IV Sent., d. 15, p. II, a. 2, q. 1.

CHAPTER THREE

1. *Immortale Dei*, 1885 (*Catholic Mind*, No. 8, 1936), p. 426.

2. Pius XI, *Divini Redemptoris*, 1937 (New York, America Press, 1937), no. 29.

3. *Contra Gentiles* (Taurini, 1937), III, c. 117.

4. "The Church Today," no. 12.

5. See Max Lerner, *America as a Civilization* (New York, 1957), pp. 729–732.

6. For an explanation of the term and the difference between "sectarian" and "ecumenical" liberalism, see Thomas Neill, *The Rise and Decline of Liberalism* (Milwaukee, 1953).

7. *The Second Treatise of Civil Government*, in *John Locke: Two Treatises of Government*, ed. Thomas I. Cook (New York, 1964), ch. II, no. 4.

8. *Du Contrat Social* (Paris, 1963), Bk. II, c. VII.

9. Locke, *op. cit.*, c. II. no. 6.

10. *Ibid.*, c. VIII and IX.

11. See Carlton Hayes. *A Generation of Materialism* (New York, 1942). p. 46.

12. John Courtney Murray, S.J., "Key Themes in the Encyclical," in the America Press ed. of PT, p. 58.

13. "The Problem of the Religion of the State," in the *American Ecclesiastical Review*, May, 1951, pp. 327–352.

14. *Ibid.*

15. *Man and the State* (Chicago, 1951), pp. 9 ff.

16. Paul Woelfl, S.J., *Politics and Jurisprudence* (Chicago, 1966), pp. 93–96.

CHAPTER FOUR

1. *Poverty in America*, ed. Louis A. Ferman, Joyce L. Kornbluh, and Alan Harber (Ann Arbor, 1965).

2. David Ricardo, *Principles of Political Economy and Taxation* (London, 1960), V, 52.

3. A. Vermeersch, *Quaestiones de Justitia* (Bruges, 1904), pp. 546 ff.; Gordon George, "The Family Living Wage," in *Social Order* (Nov. 1948).

4. Abraham Schuchman, *Codetermination* (Washington, 1957), pp. 132–33; Quentin Lauer, S.J., "Comanagement in Germany," in *Social Order* (Jan., 1951).

5. AAS, 41 (1949), 283.

6. *Ibid.*, 42 (1950), 485.

7. See Herbert J. Spiro, *The Politics of German Codetermination* (Cambridge, 1958).

8. Statement of May 7, 1949, AAS 41 (1949). 283.

9. AAS 42 (1950), 485, trans. Robert J. McEwen, S.J., Eugene Burns, S.J., and Thomas Fabini, "The Problem of Unemployment," in *Review of Social Economy* (Sept., 1950), VIII, 2, 135–37.

10. Address of March 11, 1951, to Employers, Managers, and Workmen at Madrid. AAS 43 (1951), p. 213.

11. Radio address of Sept. 1, 1944, quoted in MM, 84.

12. *The Christian Doctrine of Property* (New York, 1932), pp. 18 ff.

13. "Bishops' Program of Social Reconstruction," Statement of 1919, in Huber, *Our Bishops Speak* (Milwaukee, 1952), p. 246.

14. When it is said that the term "vocational group" is not used in MM (and PT), what is meant is that these encyclicals do not use the words "ordo" or "ordines" which appear in QA to describe the groups envisaged in its proposed social reconstruction, and which have variously been translated "vocational groups," "occupational groups," or "industries and professions." MM and PT use terms which may be equivalent: "consociationes" (MM, 60, 100); "collegia" (MM, 65, 97); "coetus civium" (MM. 66); "interjecti coetus," and "interjecta corpora" (PT, 53, 64), but QA's technical phrase, "ordines," does not appear in this connection.

CHAPTER FIVE

1. "The Church Today," No. 75.

2. R. W. and A. J. Carlyle, *History of Mediaeval Political Theory in the West*, 6 vols. (London, 1903–36), Vol. III, p. 153.

3. *Summa Theologica* (Taurini, 1932), I–II, q. 105, a. 1; q. 90, a. 3; q. 95, a. 4; q. 97, a. 3, ad 3. *De Regimine Principum*, I, 6.

4. Robert Filmer, *Patriarcha*, John Locke, *Two Treatises of Government*, ed. Thomas Cook (New York, 1964), c. I, no. 1, p. 251.

5. *Immortale Dei*, p. 442; cf. also *Libertas* (1888) and *Au Milieu des Solicitudes* (1892).

6. Pius XII (*Problem of Democracy*, Christmas Message, 1944 (New York, Paulist Press), no. 11.

7. Murray, "Key Themes in the Encyclical," p. 61.

8. William Orton, *The Liberal Tradition* (New Haven, 1945), p. 12.

9. *The Encyclopedia of the Social Sciences*, V. 442, s.v. Liberty.

10. *Cambridge Modern History* (Cambridge, 1934), III, c. XXII, "Political Thought in the 16th Century."

11. Orton, *op. cit.*, p. 82.

12. *Summa Theologica*, I–II, q. 105, a. 1.

13. *De Regimine Principum*, I, 6.

14. *Loc. cit.*

15. Heinrich Rommen, *The State in Catholic Thought* (St. Louis, 1945), p. 64.

16. Emil Brunner, *Justice and the Social Order* (New York, 1945), pp. 93 and 272.

17. Louis Mercier, "Jean Jacques Rousseau and the Totalitarians," in *America*, May 15 and 22, 1943.

18. Christmas, 1944, no. 15 (Paulist Press; 1945).

19. J. Messner *Social Ethics* (St. Louis, 1949), p. 124. This definition is further developed in the revised edition (1965), pp. 123–147.

ı

CHAPTER SIX

1. Among these documents are:

Benedict XV: "Des le Debut," Exhortation to the belligerent peoples, Aug. 1, 1917 (AAS, V. 9, p. 417; trans. in H. Koenig, *Principles for Peace*, p. 229); "Pacem Dei," Encyclical on Peace and Christian Reconciliation, May 23, 1920 (AAS, V. 12, p. 209; *Principles for Peace*, p. 284).

Pius XI: "Ubi Arcano," Encyclical on the Peace of Christ in the Kingdom of Christ, Dec. 23, 1922 (AAS, V. 14, p. 674; *Principles for Peace*, p. 332); "Caritate Christi Compulsi," Encyclical on Prayer and Reconciliation, May, 3, 1932 (AAS, V. 24, p. 177; *Principles for Peace*, p. 456).

Pius XII: "Summi Pontificatus," Encyclical on the Unity of the Human Family, Oct. 20, 1939 (AAS, V. 31, p. 543; trans. America Press); "In Questo Giorno," Christmas Message, 1939 (AAS, V. 32, p. 5; trans. in H. W. Flannery, *Pattern for Peace*, p. 99); "Grazie, Venerabili," Christmas Message, 1940 (AAS, V. 33, p. 6; *Pattern for Peace*, p. 102); "Nell Alba," Christmas Message, 1941 (AAS, V. 34, p. 10; *Pattern for Peace*, p. 104); "The Problem of Democracy," Christmas Message, 1944 (trans. The Paulist Press, 1945).

American Bishops: "Statement on International Order," Nov. 16, 1944 (*Catholic Mind*, Jan. 1945); "Statement on Organizing World Peace," Apr. 14, 1945 (*Catholic Mind*, June, 1945).

2. Linus Pauling, *On the Developed and the Developing*, Occasional Paper of the Center for the Study of Democratic Institutions (Fund for the Republic, 1965), p. 3.

3. Vatican II, taking up this matter of disarmament, explicitly states that this reduction of arms isnot a unilateral operation ("The Church Today", no. 82). The right to legitimate self-defense, which implies armaments, cannot be denied to nations "as long as the danger of war

remains and there is no competent and sufficiently powerful authority at the international level" (*ibid.* no. 79).

4. *Spaceship Earth* (New York, 1966), p. 106.

5. *Man and the State*, p. 29. For a short survey of the history of the term "sovereignty" see J. Leclercq, *Leçons de Droit Naturel* (Namur, 1933), V. I. C. V.

6. Christmas Message, 1944, no. 55 (Paulist Press, 1945).

7. *De Regimine Principum*, Bk. I, c. 1.

8. *De Legibus*, Bk. II, c. 19, no. 9.

9. *Code de Morale Internationale* (Paris, 1937), nos, 12 and 32.

10. *On Coexistence*, Occasional Paper by the Center for the Study of Democratic Institutions (Fund for the Republic, 1965), p. 29.

BIBLIOGRAPHY

Abbott, Walter M., S.J., ed., *The Documents of Vatican II* (New York, 1966).

Aquinas, St. Thomas, *Summa Theologica*, emendata De Rubeis, Billuart et Aliorum notis selectis ornata (Taurini, 1932).

—— *Summa Contra Gentiles*, reimpressio XXII stereotypa (Taurini, 1937).

—— *De Regimine Principum*, ed. Joseph Mathis (Taurini, 1924).

Barrett, Donald N., ed., *The Problem of Population* (Notre Dame, Ind., 1964).

Berle, A. A., with G. C. Means, *The Modern Corporation and Private Property* (New York, 1932).

—— *Power without Property* (New York, 1959).

Blumenthal, W. Michael, *Codetermination in the German Steel Industry* (Princeton, 1956).

Brown, Harrison, and Real, James, *Community of Fear* (New York, 1960).

Brown, Leo C., S.J., "Labor-Management Cooperation," *Social Order*, Vol. 1, No. 5, May, 1951, pp. 211–223.

Calvez, Jean-Yves, *La Penseé de Karl Marx* (Paris, 1956).

Calvez, J., S.J., and Perrin, J., S.J., *The Church and Social Justice* (Chicago, 1961).

Center for the Study of Democratic Institutions (Publications resulting from the International Convocation on the Requirements of Peace, Feb., 1965). *On Coexistence, On the World Community, On the Developed and the Developing, To Live as Men: An Anatomy of Peace,* ". . . Therefore Choose Life" (New York, 1965).

Chambre, Henri, *Christianity and Communism*, trans. R. F. Trevett (New York, 1960).

Cronin, John F., S.S., *Catholic Social Principles* (Milwaukee, 1950).

———— *Social Principles and Economic Life* (Milwaukee, 1959).

———— *The Social Teaching of Pope John XXIII* (Milwaukee, 1963).

Damen, C., C.SS.R., "De Recto Usu Superfluorum," *Analecta Gregoriana*, Vol. 9, 1935 (Rome, 1935).

D'Arcy, Martin C., S.J., *Communism and Christianity* (New York, 1957).

Djilas, Milovan, *The New Class* (New York, 1959).

Drummond, William F., S.J., *Social Justice* (Milwaukee, 1955).

Eberdt, Mary Lois, C.H.M., and Schnepp, Gerald J., S.M., *Industrialism and the Popes* (New York, 1953).

Engels, Frederick, *Socialism Utopian and Scientific* (New York, 1935).

Eppstein, John, *Code of International Ethics* (Westminster, 1953), trans. of *Code de Morale Internationale* (Paris, 1937).

———— *The Catholic Tradition of the Law of Nations* (London, 1935).

Fanfani, Amintore, *Catholicism, Protestantism, Capitalism* (New York, 1935).

Ferman, Louis A., Kornbluh, Joyce L., and Haber, Allen, eds., *Poverty in America* (Ann Arbor, 1965).

Figgis, John N., "Political Thought in the 16th Century," *Cambridge Modern History*, Vol. III. Ch. XXII (Cambridge, 1934).

Flannery, Harry W., ed., *Pattern for Peace* (Westminster, 1962).

Fromm, Erich, *Marx's Concept of Man* (New York, 1961).

Galbraith, John K., *The Affluent Society* (Boston, 1958).

George, Gordon, S.J., "The Family Living Wage," *Social Order*, Vol. 1, No. 9, Nov. 1948, p. 385; and Vol. 2, No. 1, Jan. 1949. p. 23.

Gonella, Guido, *The Papacy and World Peace: A Study of the Christmas Messages of Pope Pius XII* (London, 1945).

Hales, E. E. Y., *The Catholic Church in the Modern World* (New York, 1958).

Hayes, Carlton, *A Generation of Materialism* (New York, 1942).

Hofstadter, Richard, *Social Darwinism in American Thought* (Boston, 1960).

Hook, Sidney, *From Hegel to Marx* (Ann Arbor, 1962).

Huber, Raphael M., O.F.M., *Our Bishops Speak* (Bruce, 1952).

Hughes, Emmet, *The Church and the Liberal Society* (Princeton, 1944).

Hutchins, Robert, *St. Thomas and the World State* (Milwaukee, 1949).

John XXIII, Pope, *Mater et Magistra*, Encyclical on Christianity and Social Progress, May 15, 1961 (New York, 1961).

—— *Pacem in Terris*, Encyclical on Peace on Earth, April 11, 1963 (New York, 1963).

Kennedy, Paul V., S.J., "Labor's Participation in Management: Ethical Aspects," *Review of Social Economy*, Vol. V, No. 1, June 1947, pp. 49–59.

Kelly, George A., *Overpopulation: A Catholic View* (Glenn Rock, N.J., 1960).

Koenig, Harry C., ed., *Principles for Peace* (Washington, 1943).

Kwant, Remy C., O.S.A., *Phenomenology of Social Existence* (Pittsburgh, 1965).

Lauer, Quentin, S.J., "Comanagement in Germany," *Social Order*, Vol. 1, No. 1, Jan. 1951, pp. 11–22.

Leclercq, Jacques, *Leçons de Droit Naturel*, 5 vols. (Namur): Vol. 1, *Le Fondement du Droit de la Société* (1933).

Leo XIII, Pope, *Immortale Dei*, Encyclical on the Christian Constitution of States, Nov. 1, 1885 (*The Catholic Mind*, Vol. 34, No. 21, Nov. 8, 1936).

———— *Rerum Novarum*, Encyclical on the Condition of Labor, May 15, 1891 (Washington, N.C.W.C., 1942).

Locke, John, *Two Treatises of Government*, ed. Thomas I. Cook (New York, 1964).

Maritain, J., *Man and the State* (Chicago, 1951).

———— *Moral Philosophy*, Ch. 10, "Dialectical Materialism" (New York, 1964).

———— "The Natural Law and Human Rights," *The Dublin Review*, Vol. 210, No. 421, April, 1942, pp. 116–124.

Marx, Karl, *The Communist Manifesto*, in *Capital, The Communist Manifesto and Other Writings*, ed. Max Eastman (New York, 1932).

———— *Economic and Philosophical Manuscripts of 1844*, in *Marx's Concept of Man* by Erich Fromm (New York, 1961).

Masse, Benjamin L., S.J., *The Church and Social Progress* (Milwaukee, 1966).

Messner, J., *Social Ethics*, trans. J. J. Doherty, revised ed. (St. Louis, 1965).

Miller, Raymond, C.SS.R., *Forty Years After* (St. Paul, 1947).

Millis, Walter, *Permanent Peace* (New York, 1961).

———— *A World without War* (New York, 1961).

Moody, J. N., and Lawler, J. G., eds., *The Challenge of Mater et Magistra* (St. Louis, 1963).

Murray, J. C., S.J., *We Hold These Truths* (New York, 1960).

Nagle, William J., ed., *Morality and Modern Warfare* (Baltimore, 1960).

Neill, Thomas, *The Rise and Decline of Liberalism* (Milwaukee, 1953).

Nell-Breuning, von, Oswald, S.J., *Reorganization of Social Economy*, Engl. ed. by Bernard W. Dempsey, S.J. (Milwaukee, 1953).

Newman, Jeremiah, *Co-Responsibility in Industry* (Westminster, 1955).

———— *Foundations of Justice* (Cork, 1954).

Orton, William, *The Liberal Tradition* (New Haven, 1945).

Paul VI, Pope, *Populorum Progressio*, Encyclical on the Development of Peoples, March 26, 1967 (Boston, St. Paul Ed., 1967).

Pius XI, Pope, *Casti Connubii*, Encyclical on Christian Marriage, Dec. 31, 1930 (*The Catholic Mind*, Vol. 29, No. 2, Jan. 22, 1931).

—— *Divini Redemptoris*, Encyclical on Atheistic Communism, March 19, 1937 (New York, America Press, 1937).

—— *Quadragesimo Anno*, Encyclical on Reconstructing the Social Order, May 15, 1931 (Washington, N.C.W.C., 1942).

Pius XII, Pope, "Address to the Catholic International Congresses for Social Study and Social Action," Rome, June 3, 1950. *The Catholic Mind*, Vol. 48, No. 1052, Aug. 1950, p. 507.

—— "Address to the International Union of Catholic Employers," Rome, May 7, 1949. *The Catholic Mind*, Vol. 47, No. 1039, July, 1949, p. 445.

—— *Summi Pontificatus*, Encyclical on the Unity of Human Society, Oct. 20, 1939 (New York, America Press, 1939).

—— *Democracy*, Christmas Message of 1944, trans. John B. Harney, C.S.P. (New York, Paulist Press, 1945).

—— *Sertum Laetitiae*, Encyclical on Progress and Problems of the American Church, Nov. 1, 1939 (*The Catholic Mind*, Vol. 37, No. 886, Nov. 22, 1939, p. 923).

Rommen, Heinrich A., *The State in Catholic Thought* (St. Louis, 1945).

Rousseau, Jean Jacques, *Du Contrat Social* (Paris, 1963).

Ryan, John A., *The Christian Doctrine of Property* (New York, 1932).

Sheed, F. J., *Communism and Man* (New York, 1938).

Shuchman, Abraham, *Codetermination* (Washington, 1957).

Smith, Adam, *The Wealth of Nations,* in *A Library of Universal Literature*, Vols. 16, 17, 18 (New York, 1901).

Spiro, Herbert J., *The Politics of German Codetermination* (Cambridge, 1958).

Thompson, Charles S., ed., *Morals and Missiles* (London, 1959).

Vermeersch, A., S.J., Quaestiones De Justitia, 2nd ed. (Bruges, 1904).

Wallace, Lillian P., *Leo XIII and the Rise of Socialism* (Durham, 1966).
Ward, Barbara, *The Rich Nations and the Poor Nations* (New York, 1962).
—— *Nationalism and Ideology* (New York, 1966).
—— *Spaceship Earth* (New York, 1966).
Wetter, Gustave A., S.J., trans. Peter Heath, *Dialectical Materialism* (New York, 1958).
Wild, John, *Human Freedom and Social Order* (Durham, 1959).
Willey, Basil, *The Eighteenth Century Background* (Boston, 1961).
Woelfl, Paul, S.J., *Politics and Jurisprudence* (Chicago, 1966).
Wright, John J., *National Patriotism in Papal Teaching* (Boston, 1942).